ESSENTIAL PSYCHOLOGY

General Editor
Peter Herriot

C3

GROWING UP IN SOCIETY

GW00691712

ESSENTIAL

PSYCHOLOGY

GROWING UP IN SOCIETY

Tony Booth

Methuen

First published in 1975 by Methuen & Co Ltd
11 New Fetter Lane, London EC4P 4EE
© 1975 Tony Booth
Printed in Great Britain by
Richard Clay (The Chaucer Press), Ltd
Bungay, Suffolk

ISBN (hardback) 0 416 81890 0
ISBN (paperback) 0 416 81900 1

We are grateful to Grant McIntyre of
Open Books Publishing Ltd for assistance
in the preparation of this series

Contents

Preface

Psychology books present a bewildering variety of points of view carefully substantiated by reference to a myriad of studies. Often the same study is used to support the proponents of different views. At the same time, we are expected to think of psychology as a science that, from its inception some hundred years ago, slowly but inexorably moves towards the true explanation of human and animal thought and action. However, I have a sometimes overpowering feeling that psychological insight is not confined to the small group of individuals who get paid for increasing the volume of psychological literature. Perhaps anyone who is not paid to be a psychologist might find that easy to say too, though in the age of the 'expert' some may not have the confidence to challenge their precinct. I have been astounded at the complex analysis of human problems in literature and occasionally in the cinema. I am certainly undecided whether the psychological novel or psychological journal have more to tell us about people; whether a film like Bergman's *Crys and Whispers* offers more fertile suggestions about what it means to know that one is alive and will die than an article reporting on a questionnaire study of the attitudes of old people.

A difficulty with much psychological writing is that its subject matter seems to bear little resemblance to anything remotely human. It is often about bits of people; what they see through their eyes under certain conditions, or the way they think about abstract puzzles, when and if they do think about them. I am not the only person who wonders whether a good novelist is better able to capture the subject matter of psychology than the best psychologist. I have noticed books on the psychology shelves of the library containing collections of short stories in an attempt to capture the flavour of growing up in our society.

I hope that this feeling of uncertainty will not be regarded by everyone as a total disqualification from attempting to write my own little bit of psychological literature. What I hope it will do is to convey a need for freedom of thought that is essential in trying to understand an area of human activity.

In this book, I will be attempting to tackle some of the ways of looking at people as they develop in their interactions with other people. It is a subject which, even when confined to the academic disciplines of the social sciences, seems to lurch around between psychology, sociology, anthropology and social history. If I feel that the distinctions between professional psychologists and non-professionals is rather arbitrary, then I feel even more certain that an attempt to give a purely psychological orientation to personal and social development is a straitjacket that will confine nothing of any substance. I hope to provide a framework through which we can think about the varied contributions to our understanding of the influences determining the way people grow up together. I want to prepare the reader, too, for any future sortie into the literature. At no point is it my intention to convey an impression that there is one set of people called 'experts on human development' who have all the answers to the amazingly complex issues involved in growing through our lives.

Editor's Introduction

Tony Booth shows that children do not develop as persons in isolation from the context in which they are brought up. On the contrary, the assumptions about children which different cultures make result in different forms of childrearing and educational provision. Tony Booth discusses the historical antecedents to Western industrial man's views about children, and also provides enlightening cross-cultural comparisons.

This book belongs to Unit C of *Essential Psychology*. What unifies the titles in this unit is the concept of development. It is a very rich concept, embodying as it does the notions of process and change, and the interaction of a human being with his environment throughout his life. The individual has to maintain some sort of equilibrium between the demands of the environment and his own way of constructing reality. He has to adapt to the realities of the particular culture he lives in; but at the same time, he may to able to change his environment to a certain extent. In this way, equilibrium may be maintained without compromising his own conceptual system. The concept of development is thus ideal for dealing with growing up and changing in society. We can use the phrase 'personal development' to talk both about children and about adults; this may help us to see both as people. The reader will find other conceptual frameworks in other units. They are not so much mutually contradictory as efforts to do justice to the complexities of psychology's subject matter. Coming to terms with a variety of explanatory frameworks decreases our confidence in psychology as a mature science; but perhaps it is better to be honest about what we don't know.

Essential Psychology as a whole is designed to reflect the changing structure and function of psychology. The authors are both academics and professionals, and their aim has been to introduce the most important concepts in their areas to beginning students. They have tried to do so clearly but have not attempted to conceal the fact that concepts that now appear central to their work may soon be peripheral. In other words, they have presented psychology as a developing set of views of man, not as a body or received truth. Readers are not intended to study the whole series in order to 'master the basics'. Rather, since different people may wish to use different theoretical frameworks for their own purposes, the series has been designed so that each title stands on its own. But it is possible that if the reader has read no psychology before, he will enjoy individual books more if he has read the introductions (A1, B1, etc.) to the units to which they belong. Readers of the units concerned with applications of psychology (E, F) may benefit from reading all the introductions.

A word about references in the text to the work of other writers – e.g. 'Smith, 1974'. These occur where the author feels he must acknowledge an important concept or some crucial evidence by name. The book or article referred to will be listed in the references (which double as name index) at the back of the book. The reader is invited to consult these sources if he wishes to explore topics further. A list of general further reading is also to be found at the back of each book.

We hope you enjoy psychology.

Peter Herriot

1
The contexts of development

In a book called *Growing Up in New Guinea*, Margaret Mead describes the activities, practices and experiences that shaped the development of the children of Manus, an island off the north of Australia. In another of her books, *Coming of Age in Samoa*, she relates the early life history of the people, particularly the women of a Polynesian south sea island. Anne Moody grew up as a poor black child in the southern states of America and tells her story in *Coming of Age in Mississippi: an autobiography*. Reading these accounts, one gains an overwhelming view of the vastly different experiences that have shaped the lives of people in different parts of the world and the drastically disparate ways in which different individuals have grown up within one country.

In this book I want to discuss ways of understanding personal and social development in society. I could have attempted to describe the life cycle of an average English man and woman, but complex societies like our own contain so many different groups with their own distinctive life styles that I would have found myself describing people who do not exist. I might also have given the impression that this non-existent average English development was normal and healthy, whereas the life course of others, with their own individual problems, solutions, pleasures and confusions, were to be regarded at best with a raised eyebrow. Perhaps, like Anne Moody, I could have attempted an autobiography, but I am not sure how relevant the details of my own life would be to an understanding of the lives of others. Each individual grows up in a particular social setting within a wider society. In order to understand this process, we need to think about the individual and his interactions within the particular group or subculture in which he is born and within the wider society in which his subculture has emerged.

Margaret Mead had the opportunity to revisit the island of Manus after a period of twenty-five years and to meet again as adults many of the people who had been children on her previous visit. The changes in attitudes and values on the island were tremendous, partly as a result of contacts with other cultures that had been forged during the second world war. The changes in values had radically altered the life styles of the adults and children. The children on that island had grown up against a background of circumstances occurring at a particular time in their history that would never be repeated. There are some societies or groups within societies who, because of rigidly enforced codes of behaviour and fortuitous or carefully constructed insulation from external influences, manage to maintain continuity of development from generation to generation. However, even then, the chance effects of a natural disaster or epidemic may leave its imprint on an age group that will materially distinguish the way they grow up from the others in their society.

Of course, man as an animal species shares a common biology and this sets certain limits on the ways he can develop wherever he is. All people go through a period of early dependence on others for survival, all need food and all eventually age and die. To judge by the antics of the centenarians band in Georgia, Russia, this last fact may be strongly resisted but it is not open to serious dispute. Each individual is born, too, with a unique biological inheritance which effects his interaction with his environment and places some limit on his potentialities. However, the biological limits are wide enough to permit tremendous diversity in the personal and social development of individuals.

Because of the variety of influences acting on development, our analysis must take into account the information we can derive from disciplines other than psychology. The boundaries between the disciplines of the social sciences are blurred, just as the subjects of the secondary school curriculum are often artificially divided. To understand how the individual grows in his interrelationship with others in a group in society, we can look to psychology with its stress on the study of individuals and small groups; anthropology which involves the study and comparison of the ways of life of people in different parts of the world; social history, with its examination of the way the social fabric and life styles of individuals in one country have changed over the years; and sociology, which examines the organization of society and its influence on the behaviour of groups within the society. Eventually, we may have a model of human development that transcends these different subject areas.

The pace of human development

One way of summarizing the influences on development has been presented by Neugarten and Datan (1973). They viewed the pace at which individuals progress through the life cycle by reference to three factors: life time, social time and historic time. I have added the notion of biological time as well as a consideration of the views which describe universal cognitive or psychological stages as determining limits on an individual's wider development.

Biological time
Every individual follows his own course of biological maturation and change. When he begins to walk, run, reach sexual maturity, visibly age and weaken, he presents himself and others with problems and challenges to which adjustments have to be made. These changes may or may not be convenient to those

13

around him. The child who starts to walk at nine months may present a serious problem to a mother whose previous child has just started to walk at two years. A six foot tall young lady of fifteen from Denmark recently arrived in this country with the title, 'Miss Plenty', to promote a festival of pornography at a time when some of the other children in her school class are still interested in white mice. We shall see how different societies react in characteristically different ways to the signs of physical change as people develop and age. The ravages of biological time have held very different significance for men and women in this society, with the clientele of beauty clinics being made up by a preponderance of women.

The ageing process may exert a pressure on the timing of childbirth in one of three ways. The final limit is set by the menopause after which childbearing is impossible; secondly, women may wish to have children at a time when they will feel energetic and active while their offspring are young; thirdly, a woman may be aware that if she begins having children late in life she runs an increased risk of producing a child with a physical disorder.

Changes and variations in biological pace. Biological pace has represented a changing context of development over the years and varies considerably from one country to another (Tanner, 1968). The two measures of biological development most amenable to statistical recording have been those of height and the age of first menstruation. Since records have been kept at the beginning of the nineteenth century, height has shown a steady increase and menarcheal age a corresponding decrease.

Table 1.1 shows a typical comparison for the height of girls and boys in Sweden for the years 1938 and 1883.

We can see that the differences in height at age eleven are considerably greater than those at nineteen. Over the last hundred years children have matured in height earlier and have reached their full height sooner. At the turn of the century in Europe and America, adults did not reach their full height until they were twenty-six, but they are now fully

14

grown by eighteen or nineteen. The biological pace of development in height has increased.

This earlier maturation is similarly reflected in the figures for menarcheal age. In Europe and America, menarche appears

Table 1.1

	Girls			Boys		
	Year				Year	
	1938	1883			1938	1883
	ft. in.	ft. in.			ft. in.	ft. in.
Age 11 years	4 9	4 4	Age 11 years		4 9	4 4
Age 19 years	5 4	5 3	Age 19 years		5 9	5 7

an average of two-and-a-half to three-and-a-half years earlier than it did a hundred years ago.

The general trends in height and menarcheal age conceal considerable variations between groups. People in the poorer economic groups of this country have been consistently shorter and these differences have persisted up to the present day. Records from Manchester in 1820 show that the menarche for middle and upper class girls occurred at an average of 14·6 years, but at 15·7 years for working class girls. Socio-economic differences in onset of puberty do not persist today and this tends to occur at an average of 13 years in all groups in this country. Considerable urban-rural differences have been shown in the data from some countries. In 1880 in Poland, girls in Warsaw began menstruating at 14·8 years, but not until they were over 17 in rural areas.

The cultural variations in various parts of the world are even more striking. The Bundi of New Guinea have an average menarcheal age of 18·8 years whilst in Cuba it is 12·3 years.

Various explanations have been proposed for these changes. Nutritional factors are clearly important as is the gradual eradication of many childhood diseases. Where diets have improved children grow taller earlier and seem to menstruate sooner. The extreme food shortages in Moscow during the second world war produced thirteen-year-olds that were an inch shorter than children at the same age five years previously. There has also been some suggestion that the general climatic improvements from 1850 to 1940 accelerated the change towards earlier maturation, though there seems to be little correspondence between early maturation and warmth of climate in different parts of the world. Another point of view has been that early menstruation has been influenced by attitudes to sex. This may be an interesting suggestion but it is extremely difficult to think of a way of proving it. Perhaps you can think of one.

Research has led to apparently clear evidence on the influence of out-breeding on the height of offspring. The full grown sons of parents of different Swiss villages have been found to be an inch taller than the sons of parents from the same village. The Hutterites are an isolated sect in North America and in this group it has been found that the children of first cousins are 1·4 inches shorter than those of unrelated adults. This 'hybrid vigour', as mating between unrelated adults is called, has been attributed by some to the greater social mobility produced by the bicycle. Whatever other effects it may have, incest would seem to stunt the growth of any offspring.

Another suggested explanation for some of the height differences between adults has been proposed by Landauer and Whiting (1964). They have related height differences in different cultures to the degree of stimulation that the infant receives. Methods of binding which restrict the infant's freedom and perceptual isolation tend to produce smaller adults. Evidence in support of their explanation comes from studies on rats which have demonstrated that any high degree of stimulation given to baby rats, such as electric shock, gives rise to larger mature animals.

When we think of the stages of life of different periods in the recent past and in different parts of the world, we have to bear in mind the changing and varying patterns of biological development. There are clearly very different psychological and social pressures on a twelve-year-old that has reached puberty from one who will not reach that biological stage for

16

another four years. However, to illustrate just how difficult it is to interpret these findings, we can look at the admittedly scanty evidence that is available for menarche prior to the nineteenth century. The affluent classes in Roman times seem to have reached puberty at about thirteen years. In sixteenth century France one writer placed puberty for girls between twelve and thirteen. Support for early puberty prior to the eighteenth century comes, too, from literature of the period. The advance in the age of puberty seems to represent a restoration of the developmental timing which prevailed in the past (Dubos, 1972).

Biological development takes place against a background of the whims of nature and fortune. These figures imply that, biologically, the thirteen-year-old of today is the fifteen-year-old of a hundred years ago. Early biological maturation, however, does not seem to affect the total course of development. There is no evidence that early puberty leads to early death and there is some evidence that menopause is actually delayed when puberty is advanced.

Life time

Societies differ too in the attention they pay to the exact age of a person. Chronological age is only loosely related to the major changes that occur in the body as a result of biological maturation. In our society, we often rigidly adhere to an age pattern and this is formalized in granting legal rights at particular ages. Schools are geared to an exact range and there is a particular gain in status felt by children as each year passes. After a certain point, there is a very complex inter-relationship between age and status and the way the individual experiences the passing of time. The Jewish ritual of Bar Mitzvah is related to the thirteenth birthday of boys, irrespective of other signs of impending physical maturity.

One way that age exerts a pressure on development is in terms of the number of years that the individual feels he has left to live. People are aware that the average life expectancy is seventy years for women and sixty-five for men. The fifty-year-old man may find it hard to embark on a plan that will

17

bear fruit after twenty years. The eighteen-year-old will probably feel more inclined to embark on a political activity that he can expect (or hope) will bring results much later in his life. Time left before death has always been a potent factor in controlling the actions of individuals and it is not surprising that the forces for social change often come from young people.

Social time

Societies use the changes that occur as a result of biological maturation or increasing chronological age to delineate particular periods of development. Anthropologists use the term age-grading to refer to this process. When we talk of stages in the life cycle, it is often social time that governs these distinctions within limits set by maturation and ageing. The boundary between commonly defined stages of infancy, childhood, adolescence and old age are fixed by the conventions of society. Whilst the onset of adolescence may be loosely related to puberty, its termination may occur by the achievement of legal maturity at eighteen, by marriage, or possibly by entry into the labour force.

There is a tendency to think of stages of the life cycle commonly distinguished in one society as having a universal psychological significance for all societies at all times. For example, the first menstruation marks a biological stage for all girls and is likely to provoke some measure of psychological change in the girls of all societies. However, there is a vast difference in the ways societies regard the event. In some it is virtually ignored and there appears to be little change in individual developmental continuity; in others it signifies a complete change in status, from girl to woman, and involves the adoption of a new range of activities. The Incas of Peru delineated ten separate stages for boys alone, each stage of life being associated with a particular function in that society (Linton, 1942). In many societies the system of age-grading is used to mark the point when another part of the cultural heritage is passed on to the rising generation.

One way of marking social changes in the life cycle is by

reference to membership of particular institutions. I heard a headteacher of an infant school wishing a child happy birthday in front of the rest of the school. After asking the child her age and receiving the reply 'Six', the headteacher asked, 'And what will you be next year?' 'A junior', replied the little girl. We talk of the nursery school child, the infant, the junior, the senior and the working boy and girl with the implication that membership of each new institution heralds a new stage in the development of the individual. Gordon Lowe (1972) wrote 'We have quite arbitrarily chosen to regard old age as starting around sixty-five, the usual age of retirement.' However there is nothing arbitrary about marking the social stage of old age by reference to the leaving of a work organization.

The stages of the life cycle which are delineated within a particular society represent a clock against which individuals can measure their own development. Each individual becomes aware of the cultural expectations governing a particular stage or event in the cycle and may be aware that he is lagging behind and make efforts to catch up. Even where there is no formal enforcement of a progression, the age-grade exerts a pressure to conformity which may shape the life cycle.

Historic time

Each child is born into a setting that is characterized by a particular set of political, economic, and social events and institutions. These make up a constantly changing background against which life is lived. When we study a sample of a particular age group, called a cohort, and follow their social development over a number of years in a longitudinal study (see C1 of *Essential Psychology*), we become, in a sense, social historians who have looked at an interaction that can never be repeated. This provides another reason, besides the time consuming and costly nature of the enterprise, why longitudinal studies are seldom replicated or why replications after a period of time may yield results which do not correspond with the original study.

We can think of societies as comprised of a set of age strata which, because of their unique historic experiences are characterized by particular patterns of behaviour in work and in consumption, in religion, marriage, child-rearing and leisure. The political and economic situation within a society will be a factor in determining the ages of entry and departure from the work force and the numbers of individuals who escape from a struggle for the basic necessities of life. Population bulge may impose conditions of overcrowded schools and housing and be another factor affecting competition for employment. Difficulties in finding independent housing may produce a delay in the age of marriage and lead the particular cohort to have fewer children.

Use might have been made, for example, of our knowledge of the effect on the balance of population of the first world war, with its fantastic toll on the lives of young men of that period. Careful consideration of significant influences on an age stratum such as this might lead to predictions of the social needs of these individuals as they progress to old age. In research into the way in which attitudes change with age, we have to take care to distinguish the effect that may be attributed to processes associated with increasing age from those determined by influences that are specific to a cohort. Thus conservatism in a group of old people may be due to their specific educational experiences, rather than necessarily signifying an age trend that will be repeated by the next generation.

Parents always rear children in a social context which they have never before experienced themselves. Part of the so-called 'generation gap' is produced by successive generations being formed by different constellations of influences.

Population trends. The population structure in a society at a particular time, may have a considerable influence on the course of development. Every society is composed of a characteristic age structure determined by the relative size of the varying age groups in its population. In industrialized societies there are always at least three age categories: an adult producer and dependent young and old people (Bossard and Boll, 1966). The age structure of a particular society is affected by the birth rate, the death or survival rate, and the rates of migration and immigration. Any trends in overall population have to be considered in the light of these three factors.

Table 1.2 Age groups as a percentage of the population

Age group	1971	1871
Under 5	8·1%	13·7%
65+	12·8%	5·1%

Adapted from *Census Reports Annual Abstracts of Statistics*

The figures in Table 1.2 illustrate some of the major population changes in England from the years 1871–1971. There has been a decline in the numbers of children under five, despite a massive increase in infant survival rates. There has also been a vast increase in the population over sixty-five years produced by a declining death rate. This has considerable implications for the lives of young children, adults and old people, in terms of the childrearing obligations, the opportunity for relationships with others of a similar age, and the demands on society for the care and support of the elderly.

The changing survival rates, birth rates and increase in longevity, have produced an entirely different pattern of development over the last hundred years. Marriages now last an average of ten years longer than they did at the turn of the century. In 1890 the last child married about two years after the death of one parent, whereas in 1950 the last child married between thirteen and fourteen years before the death of either parent (Nimkoff, 1963).

Cognitive and psychological time
Some theorists have argued that there are universal stages of development for all individuals. Two principal examples involve the theories propounded by Piaget on the sequence of the emergence of thought processes in the child (C2) and the Freudian notion of stages of psychosexual development (D3). Both these approaches maintain that the progression of

21

the child through the sequence of stages, depends upon his having completed the previous stage and that each stage involves the child in an entirely different set of preoccupations. The rate at which children pass through the stages sets limits on the ways in which they interact with other people. I do not intend to embark on a lengthy critique of these theories here. However, some examples may serve to illustrate how the notions of the invariant sequence of stages can be applied to personal and social development.

Piagetian theory. Piaget identified the sensorimotor, pre-conceptual, intuitive, concrete operational and formal operational stages in the development of thought processes. Kohlberg (1969) has developed a theory of moral development which is based on a Piagetian approach. He argues, for example, that before the age of six or seven, a child is not able to put himself in the position of another child. His ideas of morality are based on the notions of obedience and punishment. However, by the age of about seven, during Piaget's period of concrete operations, he is able to do mental experiments which enable him to achieve an idea of how others might feel in similar situations. He develops the notion of reciprocity: 'if he hits me, I can hit him back'; 'if I hit him he can hit me back'. In the area of sex-role development, the child of two knows he is called a boy or girl, but tends to use words as proper names. It is not until he has achieved a notion of classes and categories that he can begin to see himself as a member of the group of children called girls or boys and then begin to identify with that group.

Freudian theory. On the Freudian view the child moves through a succession of stages known as the oral, anal, phallic, oedipal, latency and pubertal stages. Identification with members of one's own sex can occur only as a resolution of the oedipal stage in the fourth or fifth year of life during which the child regards the same-sexed parent as a rival for sexual gratification from the opposite-sexed parent. Resolution of this conflict occurs by identification with the same-sexed

22

parent and adapting the direct need for sexual gratification to one of vicarious fulfilment. If the conditions for favourable resolution of the conflict are not present then the child is unable to progress to the next stage of development. In writing of Freud's notion of the incestuous feelings between parents and children, I am assuming that familiarity with these opinions has reduced what has been termed 'Freud shock', with which listeners to his lectures were sometimes afflicted.

I am not suggesting that the stages mentioned here are universal for all children in all cultures, I am merely pointing out the way this approach can be seen to affect the pace of human development. Nor does the notion of cognitive or psychological stage preclude the notion of social stage. Some societies grant adult status to individuals during a period of special instruction in the beliefs and values of their culture. One might maintain that this social stage could not occur until the individual had passed through a cognitive stage in which he was able to grasp general principles that would guide his behaviour in situations in which he was not immediately involved. Cognitive or psychological stage, like events in biological maturation or the passing of the years, can be considered as forming a structure on which society can build its own pace of development.

Age and human development

Human development has been commonly defined as physical and psychological changes that occur with increasing age. It is this focus that has led to descriptions of the psychology of the average two-year-old, three-year-old, eighteen-year-old. Our discussion of biological time, social time, historic time and cognitive and psychological time, indicates that what happens to an individual at a particular age can only be understood in terms of the particular processes affecting him at a certain time. In the absence of a knowledge of these processes, a person's age tells us relatively little about his psychological state. We live in a society that keeps careful records of dates of birth and which confines children, in a year system at school, to social interactions with others of their own age. We then regard it as abnormal if a child of ten enjoys playing with eight-year-olds. I have often heard parents and teachers speak of a child as immature or precocious, because he or she enjoys being with older or younger children. Yet by the age of fifteen, it is culturally acceptable for a boy to accompany a girl two years younger in age.

Group differences

There are several problems that emerge in looking for age trends in behaviour. A general age trend in a sample of the population may conceal differences between groups of children. Each subculture has a pattern of experiences which affects the pace of development. Boys and girls can be considered as different subcultures in society for which there are distinctive expectations about age appropriate behaviour. These expectations are in their turn affected by the other groups to which a particular boy or girl belongs. In working class culture, the fifteen-year-old girl may be three years from an expected life as a wife and mother, while middle class values might lead one to predict another seven years as a single girl.

Describing and explaining age trends

A second problem arises when we use a description of an age trend as an explanation of the change. We have seen how changes with age may reflect the different history of experiences that have affected a particular age group. Adults who were children during the second world war may have been influenced by the absence of fathers and incredible stresses during early childhood in ways that distinguish them from younger people. These differences occur because of different historic experiences, not just because there is an age difference in the two groups. In looking at the age of development of specific friendships in children, we might find a dramatic increase in relationships after five years of age. We could conclude that at five, children were most ready to make specific friendships. However, this would overlook the impact of school and the opportunities it provides for establishing friends and, incidentally, for becoming an 'isolate'.

When we discover a series of changes associated with increasing age, we have to look for an explanation in terms of the biological, social, historical or psychological process by which it is determined. Chronological age is merely a measure of the time during which diverse processes can occur and is a 'variable that will not be required in advanced theories of development' (Gewirtz, 1969).

Prospect

We have looked at various factors which affect the way an individual develops. It is my thesis that radically different experiences produce 'real' differences between people; that people born in poverty and who die early after a perpetual struggle for existence have a personal and social development that is incomparably different from that of a child born in a wealthy middle class suburb of London. The readership of this book may find this patently obvious, yet writers in psychology have sometimes minimized the differences that occur. When a psychologist writes 'Fundamentally men are alike the world over', (Nash, 1970) he is expressing an opinion about what could constitute a fundamental difference between people. Of course, basic biological similarities may mean that any group of babies from anywhere could be adapted to any particular culture. Yet as things are, extreme differences between cultures produce differences in the style and quality of life that are a vivid reality to those experiencing them.

2
The individual and society

To understand social and personal development, we need to investigate the concepts used to explain how an infant grows up to fit in with his society. The challenge offered to society by the continual birth of new members has been likened to an 'incessant invasion of barbarians'. The term socialization was developed by sociologists to explain how vast numbers of humans are able to adjust their behaviour to one another, to maintain an ongoing social order. It has been defined in various ways depending on the interests of the writers and the subject discipline to which they belong. On one definition it is 'the process by which someone learns the ways of a given society or social group, so that he can function within it' (Elkin and Handel, 1972). A more psychological flavour was given to the concept by Child (1954): 'Socialization is the process by which an individual born with behaviour potentialities of an enormously wide range is led to develop actual behaviour confined within the narrow range of what is customary for him according to the standards of his group.'

Some sociologists, impressed by the way a social order could be maintained over the years, conceived of society as an integrated set of economic, political and social organizations. They thought of the socialization process as carefully shaping individuals so that they could be slotted into their appropriate positions in the system. The network of institutions in society was maintained because each organization had developed to fulfil the needs of the individuals and other organizations. Thus institutions and individuals were locked together by a stable interdependence. The 'structural-functionalist' view, as it was called, led to a notion of societies as relatively static and unchanging.

However, it is clear that there are disparate wishes and conflicting organizations in most societies, with a balance of power between groups that is sometimes stable and sometimes precarious. Any view of socialization must allow for the possibility of social change, either as a gradual process or as a result of violent revolution. In complex societies then, we must conceive of the socialization process as occurring in the first instance within the particular subcultures or groups in which the child is born. At birth he may be a member of a social class, ethnic, geographical and sex group for which he will have to learn particular patterns of behaviour. He will also have to learn the patterns of relationships of these groups with others in society.

Institution, role and status
We can think of a society as comprised of a set of organizations or institutions. These include schools, hospitals, factories, churches, pubs as well as the family. Each organization can be described in terms of the positions occupied by its members, the behaviour that is expected of someone in a particular position and the function that an institution performs in relation to other institutions in the society. The barman in a pub is expected to serve beer ('sorry sir, no beer, but we've plenty of cheese'), the customer to ask for it and pay for it

('No cheese thanks, but I could do with a new pair of underpants. I'll give you my socks in part-exchange.') The position in an institution is sometimes called a *status* and the expected behaviour a *role*. For any status, we can specify the rank or power with which it is associated. Our barman has the right to ask a customer to leave the pub. While this sort of analysis suggests that we can make generalizations about the institutions in a society, we have to be aware of the possible variations that can occur. The family in 'our' society may be said to consist of a father, mother and children with power or rank occurring in descending order. However, who 'rules the roost' will vary from family to family and there may be other important family members, such as grandparents or a totally different childrearing structure on a commune.

Norms and values

In any particular situation, appropriate patterns of behaviour may be defined and confined by a set of *norms* or rules determined by a set of general principles or *values*. The value that one should 'give as good as one gets' may be applied in a particular situation in terms of a sharp verbal retort or a punch in the face, which represents the norm for a particular group of people. As we have seen the norms, values, statuses and roles confronting a child initially will be those specific to his own social milieu. Soon, however, he will come to learn something about the institutions in the wider society.

Social class and subculture

In societies there is a system of allocating status, wealth or both, which may be associated with the type of work that one does. In Western society, the notion of socio-economic class defines this status pattern. At the top of the ladder are the professions, who have replaced the nobility in England. At the 'bottom' are the unskilled manual workers. In India, the caste system, particularly in former times, determined the socializing experiences one would receive, the work one would be permitted to do and one's future wealth or poverty.

Clearly, a society must have some way of allocating jobs.

Not everyone can become a brain-surgeon or a dustman even if they wanted to; there are only a limited number of vacancies in each of these categories. This allocation can be conducted as in the Indian caste system or in the English feudal structure by a rigid adherence to limits determined at birth. On the other hand, we can attempt to provide equal opportunity in terms of a universal school-system, in which job allocation depends, to a certain extent, on examination results. However, once a particular class or caste system is in operation, it takes a social and political revolution to completely eradicate its influence, for the roles that the adults in a particular subculture pass on to their children will tend to be those in which they themselves are involved. Each social class group will entertain, too, a set of attitudes towards other groups and a set of expectations about themselves that will tend to perpetuate the class structure. A child whose father is a doctor, will be expected by others to do well at school and will anticipate success himself. His socialization experiences will be directed towards maintaining continuity in his family class or status position from father to son. In English society, the two opposing pressures produced by the removal of job allocation from birth to school and the subcultural socialization influences permit a certain degree of change from one class group to another. However, this change, or *social mobility*, is not as great as would occur if children had truly equal opportunities.

The patterns of social class-related behaviour which have their roots in the English feudal structure produce fairly pervasive differences in socializing influences. Groups differ in terms of their child-rearing methods, their leisure activities and patterns of social and sexual relationships. Some of these differences are related to differences in wealth, whilst others are produced by the historical pressures acting on the particular group. We can talk of subcultures to distinguish groups that exhibit characteristic differences.

Related to the social class structure of the society is the particular racial or ethnic group to which one belongs. In this country, the influx of black immigration in the 1950s to fill some of the lower paid jobs created a group that have found social mobility particularly difficult to achieve. In contrast with immigration of other white groups, earlier in the century, skin colour has served as a potent feature with which to associate a particular set of attitudes and opportunities. In the United States, attempts have been made to alter the influence of the black ghetto culture, associated with appalling poverty and housing conditions and a history of particular expectations and attitudes, by bussing children from city centre 'black' schools to 'white' schools. In the light of our discussion on the effects of socialization in producing and perpetuating subcultures, such limited attempts at social change would seem to be futile.

Social class and the position of women in society. Some writers have argued that a division of labour between men and women was the earliest form of social class separation in society and that this division formed the basis for the exploitation of women by men and for all other exploitative relationships (Firestone, 1972). There is little doubt that the subjection of women by the authority of men has often placed them in an invidious position in our society. They remained deprived of the right to vote long after this had been granted to the working class population. They were initially banned from membership of the male-dominated unions and this contributed to the unfair deal they have received from employers in the past. Their position of 'domestic slavery' has only recently been recognized as entitling them to a joint share in the property of their family.

However there is no need to regard the battle of the sexes as the most basic exploitative relationship. In many societies men have always exploited animals and 'nature'. It is interesting that when Shulamith Firestone argues the case for freeing women from their biological nature she calls for a 'revolutionary ecological programme that will realize the original goal of empirical science: human mastery of matter.' Unfortunately the careless exploitation of nature may produce problems in the near future that far outweigh those raised by class or sex conflicts.

Defining 'society'

The term society is a vague one. It is less precise than the term country. When, for example, we speak of Western society, we tend to refer to the similarities that exist between industralized countries, which have a largely urban culture. This issue is particularly pertinent to psychology, where English and American research has tended to develop a shared literature. We rarely talk of cross-cultural studies in comparing experiments in these two countries, yet there are obviously important differences between English and American cultures.

Goals and agencies of socialization

The concepts we have used in describing the structure of society can be seen to represent the *goals* of the socialization process. During this process, the individual is prepared for the statuses he will occupy in the organizations in his society and is taught the role behaviour appropriate to each status. Satisfactory performance of each role involves the acquisition of a set of habits, beliefs, attitudes and needs. He will also learn the way his own group and subculture fit in with the wider society.

Agencies of socialization

At a particular point in the development of a society, the job of teaching and maintaining role behaviour is conducted by organizations that have been termed *agencies* of socialization. Agencies of socialization that are prominent in our society for most people at present, are the family, school, peer group, mass-media and work situation. Groups within society are influenced to different degrees by church, pub and dance hall. At different points in our lives, other institutions such as hospitals, mental asylums, prisons and old age homes may teach us entirely new ways of behaving which may be either specific to our stay in the institution or may affect our lives subsequently. *Agents* of socialization are individuals within an organization who have the task of teaching people their roles in their present situations and preparing them for the future roles they will need in situations appropriate to later stages of their lives. For example, a parent teaches an infant the set of behaviours appropriate to his age, sex, and birth order in the family. At the same time, the child has to be prepared for the roles demanded by relationships with friends and by entry into school.

The notions of organizations, status, role, norms, values and agency of socialization give us one way of describing the way significant social settings shape an individual's development at a particular time in a subculture of a given society. In different societies or at different times within the same society, different organizations become prominent as agencies of socialization that prepare and maintain an individual's role behaviour. It may help to give a picture of these influences if we consider in a little more detail some of our principal agencies of socialization. We will take a further look at the way they have emerged historically in Chapter 4. I have stressed that the notion of agencies of socialization may involve us in making generalizations about institutions that will not always apply to a particular situation. It is because agencies and agents of socialization differ that the socializing experiences of individuals are never the same. Agencies and agents of socialization produce the differences in people, as well as their similarities.

Family
The family presents the infant with its first image of society in the context of its particular subcultural settings. The pattern of relationships that he meets serves as a first, but powerful glimpse of the possible interactions between people. During the first year of life he is likely to develop *attachments* to other members of the family that may have profound effect on his ability to make relationships with others. He may also learn that it is possible for him to lead an independent existence. It is almost certain that the child will learn a set of behaviours appropriate to his or her sex. From the moment of birth, boys and girls are treated differently by parents,

brothers and sisters. Although much of our sex-role behaviour may be 'personally constricting', it is maintained and enhanced by institutions throughout our lives.

Like all agencies of socialization, the family exerts a socializing influence on all its members. It induces parents to exhibit new role behaviour, which radically alters their lives.

School

The school introduces the child to the wider society where there are new patterns of authority and new possibilities for forming relationships. Even where there is no emphasis on competition at home, he will become aware that individuals are valued differently depending on what they can do. He will no longer be valued just for what he is. Generally he will be age-graded within the narrow confines of his year of birth and will tend to seek out similar age-mates. As he progresses through the school, at some point he will learn that his society has a pyramidal structure with a few places at the top, but with most people destined for a lower status. The final years of schooling may perform functions of *allocation* of a child to a particular occupational role.

Peer group

The peer group or association of age-mates is produced to a great extent, by the age-grading of the school. It is a vague concept which can refer to two or three friends, to the general influence of a school class, to gang membership, or to the mutual interactions of an amorphous mass of young people at a football crowd. Such groups bring together the socializing influences of various families within limits set by a tendency for children to make friends with others from similar backgrounds. It may provide a particular child with a larger setting in which to exert influence. It may also enable the child to resist, through solidarity and support from friends, the socializing pressures of adults, such as teachers and parents. In changing societies, the peer group may enable the child to practise roles that he will need in his future life, which his parents have been unable to teach him. Such groups are altered considerably by a child's development of sexual interests, his movement out of the age-restricted school environment into the labour force and by socializing pressures involved in starting a family. By and large, the gangs which serve as a base for delinquent activities, are disbanded in this way and do not lead to adult criminality.

Work organizations

On entry into the labour market, the individual meets one of the most powerful and impersonal socializing agents; money. The potency of a particular job in shaping the attitudes and behaviour of people will depend on the economic situation. When jobs are scarce, people will be prepared to conform to a work situation which they might have seen as incompatible with their attitudes in easier times. Work organizations exert most influence as socializing agencies in societies which have developed job specialization. In rural economies where the family works together, as a work unit, no distinction can be drawn between family and occupational socialization.

The way in which organizations can attempt to influence the attitudes of new recruits can be illustrated by reference to a talk that was given to trainees in a social work department. The head of the department explained that the employees had three duties. Their first duty was to their employers, their second to the social work profession, and only last of all did he mention their obligation to the customers or clients in need of their services. The adoption of the aims of organization that have been at variance with one's previous attitudes has been termed institutionalization. Often the adoption of a particular set of attitudes is a precondition for material advancement in the organization.

Mass media

The mass media include television, radio, newspapers and advertising. A considerable amount has been written about the impact of television on the lives of individuals; on the effects of permissive sex and indiscriminate violence on the screen. The average viewing time for children in England was fourteen hours a week sixteen years ago (Himmelweit, 1958). At a similar time, the young American viewer was watching for twenty-two hours (Bailyn, 1959). We will look at some possible effects when we discuss the power of models for imitation. The 'media' serve to keep the individuals in a society in touch with changing social trends and constantly affect the attitudes and values of people of all ages. In placing people in touch with the values of others in different parts of their country or the world, the media create possibilities for understanding others and also serve as a potent reminder to the have-nots that others are better off than they are.

We saw in the previous chapter how each society creates a series of age-status changes. One of the functions of the media has been to create and enhance different patterns of need and consumption for different age-groups that become obsolete as the individual ages. In the United States, styles of clothing and records aimed at different age-groups have produced the new stages of life of the 'teeny' and 'weeny bopper'.

Other agencies of socialization

The pub in England is an underrated force in maintaining patterns of social role behaviour. The pattern of licensing hours and the rules prohibiting children under eighteen have facilitated the separation of men from their families at drinking time. It is totally different, in this respect, from the cafe in other countries. The dance hall used to rate in this country as the place where the majority of people met their future marriage partners. The church may have reduced in political influence, but it still exerts a considerable influence over the pattern of social relationships of a large number of people. The type of housing provided for individuals causes or maintains their development along certain directions and it may be worth considering housing patterns as a socializing agency. Suburban houses tend to limit children and parents to an interaction within their own families and create and enhance the roles of home-handyman for the owner-occupier. Life in flats may socialize individuals into tolerating later roles, which allow them little privacy. Individual family housing units have created the specific role of housewife for women which has led to problems of surburban isolation for mothers of very young children. 'We shape our buildings and afterwards our buildings shape us' (Winston Churchill).

Interrelationship between agencies of socialization

Each organization expects to receive individuals prepared for their specific roles by the agent of socialization that has preceded them and in this way exert a force for control. Head-teachers of schools complain when the teacher training colleges produce teachers whose role behaviour does not conform to the expectations of the school organization and when schools catering for lower age-groups send in pupils who do not perform in the anticipated way. The forces for social change act unevenly within the institutions of society and produce this constant friction between organizations.

The individual as a socializing agent

During our discussion of agents and agencies of socialization, I may have given an impression that the individual is passively shaped by socializing pressures from his parents, school and place of work. I intend to correct any such impression now. From the moment of his birth the human infant exerts a profound influence in the course of his own development.

In C1 of *Essential Psychology* Harry McGurk pointed out the ways in which ideas of the nature of the mind of a new born child have changed. At different times the infant's mind has been considered as totally blank, as inherently evil and naturally good. These views have cropped up in various forms over the years but the predominant view now sees an infant as born with his own set of dispositions and predispositions that he acquires from his genetic inheritance, the conditions of life inside the womb and the nature of his birth.

Even if all babies were born with a mind that was formed only by events occurring after birth, they would still be strongly influential in shaping their own development. Throughout their lives the adult caretakers of a child have been socialized into producing particular pattern of behaviour associated with the birth. Men and women learn the roles of 'father' and 'mother' during the course of their own socializing experiences; I would suggest that maternal and paternal behaviour would persist, in our society, even if there were no biological releasing mechanisms to determine their occurrence. The birth of an infant sparks off a chain of behaviour that tends to keep its parents in a stable situation. Its physical size, its facial appearance and especially its sex determine a particular pattern of parental response. As it develops its own individual personality, it will constantly provoke complex interactions and reactions from caretakers whose own personal development will be affected considerably.

The presence of a genetic and prenatal endowment adds further to the socializing power of the infant. The way it cries, the extent of its crying, the timing of its first smile, whether it smiles or laughs frequently, will all have their effects. The inherited dispositions of a child will produce variations in its temperament which interact with the experiences it receives. One writer was so impressed by the child's influence that she regards the parents as far more passive than the child in their mutual interactions (Rheingold, 1969). However, the importance of the child's individuality in provoking changes in its parents will depend on their willingness to be responsive to its idiosyncratic behaviour. It will come as no surprise to discover that the power of the infant as a socializing agent may vary from culture to culture and in different historical periods.

What applies for the infant in the family applies equally to the individual in all his situations. The degree of his influence will, of course, depend on the rigidity of the roles and statuses of a particular institution that he chooses to join or joins from necessity. To the extent that the individual is able to choose his own situations, he can determine the socializing influences that he would like to operate on him. Within the confines of their subculture and economic situation all individuals make plans and work out strategies which affect the course of their lives.

Institutions and individual development

The individual has a certain degree of freedom in shaping his own development. This freedom is limited by the forces determining his subcultural socialization and by the total pattern of institutions in his society. Institutions in a society may vary considerably, yet the variations may be based on a central theme or be carefully monitored by a centralized bureaucracy. The man who wishes to adopt a life style in which he is involved in all the decisions which affect his working life will find very few situations in which to express this view. The teacher in the state school system will similarly find it impossible to live a daily life based on the equality of status of all individuals working together. The schoolchild who decides that he would rather spend his time in other ways than attending lessons will need to have access to academically qualified adults and be prepared to examine the 1944 education act very carefully if he is to avoid the attempts at legal enforcement of school attendance.

John Holt (1974) described the outcome of some informal discussion he had with children in various schools in America. He asked young secondary school children if they would like to spend some of their time living away from their families and every hand shot up in the air. Yet most of these children had little opportunity to exercise any choice in where they lived.

When an individual finds that he does not match the demands of institutions that would normally provide him with an adequate regular income he may 'drop out' of the existing social system. He is then faced with forming new social relationships outside the common situations for meeting others and may need to search out other people with similar attitudes who are willing to attempt alternative solutions to the basic issues of acquiring food, housing, companionship and enjoyment.

The early development of social behaviour can be considered as laying the foundation for socialization. The initial basis for all socialization is the presence of communication or 'social signal systems' between the child and adults (see B1 and B2). Through their mutual communication, the child develops attachments to the adults who take care of him and in order to respond to others in his society, he must at the same time develop his own independence.

Social signals
Which social signals are emphasized in developing a child's social behaviour may vary from family to family and sub-culture to subculture. It is almost certain, however, that notice will be taken of the child's crying, its smiling and its emerging language. Other signs of a progressing relationship may involve the amount of eye-contact between child and parent and the extent to which the child will follow an adult with its eyes. As soon as he is mobile, he will express his attachment by physically following, by cuddling, clapping his hands, raising his arms in greeting and using an adult as a base for exploration (Ainsworth, 1964).

Crying
Crying refers to a number of signals that can be separately recognized by parents. Wolff (1969) identified three different patterns; the 'hungry' cry, the 'angry' cry and the 'pain' cry, which were characterized by different length of cry, timing of pauses and loudness.

These different patterns provide the parent with an opportunity of responding to the child's needs and the child with one basis on which to distinguish the adults around him, both in terms of their degree and pattern of responsiveness. Thus, he may have the basis for depending on one adult when he is hungry and another for comfort.

The crying response may serve to indicate to an adult that there is something that he or she has not done. Depending on the prior experiences of the adult and their degree of confidence in their own fathering or mothering, a persistent cry can suggest that they have failed. This is one reason why persistent crying by a child may eventually provoke a violent reaction from some parents which will produce another statistic in the baby-battering files.

Smiling

At around the sixth week of life most infants begin to smile to human faces. This initial social response then becomes a pleasure response which may be directed towards toys, the child's hand or novel objects. After about four months of age the smile may once again become primarily oriented towards people (Rheingold, 1966). The infant's smile functions as a powerful reinforcement for behaviour of parents; they tend to seek smiles from the child and frequent smiles help to maintain parent and child in close proximity. Whilst crying may act as a negative response which can serve to indicate to a parent that something needs doing, the smile serves to positively reinforce parental attachment. The prior experiences of an adult again determine his or her needs to elicit smiling and the degree to which smiling will become a dominant social signal in the emerging social relationships of her child.

Vocalization and language

The development of language represents the most powerful of the social signal systems around which can be built a pattern of reciprocal interaction between child and adult. The presence of language facilitates the learning of social roles and enables those roles which include language behaviour to be practised. It enables a child to specify his needs to a much greater degree than his crying. Associated with the development of language is a pattern of gestures and facial expression which may be specific to a particular subcultural group. Where the development of language is delayed for any reason, gesture or mime may serve, for a while, as the child's major signalling system.

The pattern of language that a child develops in his family

is often characteristic of the subculture to which the family belongs and will serve as a signal of subcultural group membership to others (see C2). When a child begins school, his style of language may well determine a set of expectations and attitudes that are associated with his group. Bernstein (1964) described some of the characteristics of middle class and working class language with the notions 'elaborated' and 'restricted' codes respectively. Labov (1970) has taken issue with this view particularly as it applies to black ghetto culture in the States. When working class blacks are met informally by other blacks, they show an ability to express a tremendous range of thought and concept. Rather than use the evaluative words 'elaborated' and 'restricted', Labov prefers to consider the language of different groups as just different. However, it is through the subcultural language that an individual learns many of his early social roles, and this may create difficulties for a child in school who is expected to respond to a different language experience.

Attachment
Through the interactions that are built around the social signal systems a child develops attachment to certain adults. Before the age of about six months, an infant shows very little distress when separated from the adults who care for him. After this period, he develops an increasing reaction to removal from his principal caretakers. This is true at least in societies that employ the relatively small family group as a socializing agent. The pattern of development of attachment may differ in groups that use communal child rearing methods, such as the Kibbutz in Israel, although Bowlby (1969) found that Kibbutz children were more attached to their mothers whom they saw every morning than the mother-substitutes who looked after the children during the day and at night. The period when the child shows preference for being cared for by a particular set of adults can be seen as a move from a stage of non-focused dependence to a stage of focused social attachment.

Some investigators believed that an attachment had to be

made specifically to a mother before a child could develop attachments to others (e.g. Bowlby, 1953). Fortunately, for the child it does seem that other attachments will serve as a basis for his social development. In a sample of Scottish children Schaffer and Emerson (1964) noted that by eighteen months of age the sole principal attachment of a child was to the mother in only half of their sample and one third of the children had a principal attachment to the father. In large families, the main caretaking of a young child may be conducted by an older sister or brother.

With the developing focus of attachment, the child also begins to differentiate between people who fulfil certain needs such as comfort, play and feeding. In any experiment which looks at a child's preference for different people, we need to know the precise detail of the situation. Schaffer (1971) has suggested that after six or seven months of age, the child develops a fear of strangers. However, this may only be true if the stranger attempts to lift the child up. If he just stands in front of the child and smiles and talks, then the baby will usually just be amused (Rheingold and Eckerman, 1973).

Independence

As soon as he can move a child will begin to explore his environment. In an unfamiliar place, he will often use an attachment figure as a base from which to discover new territory. His willingness to venture forth may depend on the quality of his attachment to the caretaker and his ability to understand that the caretaker will remain even if he or she is temporarily out of sight. Unfortunately, some authors have used the word 'detachment' to represent the child's increasing willingness to move away from a loved person (Schaffer, 1971) and this suggests that there is a weakening of the attachment bond between the two individuals. If an adult equates 'independence' with 'detachment', he may perceive the child's developing freedom as a threat to the parent-child relationship and make efforts to curb it. However, as soon as an individual is able and happy to do things away from the sight of a loved person, then he begins to develop his own 'private life'. It is at this point that children begin to have experiences which shape their lives in ways which make them different from their parents. In our society, children begin to 'grow away' from their parents in this sense when they are two years old, not as some adults believe, when they begin to make their need for independence known at the age of fifteen. The problems of 'letting go' can be faced and resolved at each stage of a child's developing independence from the socializing influences of the family.

Mechanisms for the socialization process

Since the socialization process involves learned patterns of behaviour, all theories of learning are relevant as possible mechanisms by which the goals of socialization are achieved. We shall contrast in this section the approaches associated with the names of B. F. Skinner and A. Bandura (see B1). Skinner stressed the step by step acquisition or shaping of complex behaviour by selective reinforcement or rewarding of each link in a chain of actions. Bandura has concentrated on the ability of humans to imitate complex behaviour by observing it.

Instrumental training

Instrumental conditioning or training refers to procedures, like that developed by Skinner, which increase the likelihood of repetition of a particular response by rewarding it when it happens to occur (see A3). For example, if you smile and nod your head every time someone uses a particular word, then they are very likely to say it more frequently. To be effective, the reward has to be selective. At college, the eminent social psychologist who took us for tutorials used to give us so much encouragement that we ended up producing less and less whilst still getting the same level of reward. That was the only time I had a bad end of term psychology report.

Skinner taught hungry pigeons to play a form of table

43

tennis with their beaks. At first he gave the pigeon grain whenever it chanced to touch the ball, then once the bird was regularly touching the ball for food, reward was gradually delayed until the bird had learnt that it would be fed only if it pecked the ball in a reasonably straight line across the table. Another bird placed across the table was behaviourally shaped in the same way.

We can see that complex behaviour can be gradually developed in this way and it is likely that a certain amount of social learning can occur by selectively rewarding or punishing aspects of a child's behaviour. It is this approach which has led to the development of behaviour modification techniques by which patients in a mental hospital or children in a school class have been gradually induced to develop 'socially desirable' behaviour. However, human children exhibit an astonishing ability to learn whole chunks of behaviour at a time, just by watching another person and this serves as a remarkably economical way in which to acquire role behaviour.

Imitation
Whether children have to learn to imitate or whether they are born mimics, there is little doubt that a young child may reproduce later, in his play or interactions with others, many of the scenes he has witnessed previously. He will reconstruct his parents' arguments as well as playing out the roles his parents adopt in doing housework or jobs around the house, in their reactions to him and when they meet their friends. Unlike in the instrumental conditioning situation, once a child has developed an ability to copy others, he will do so happily without any external reward or reinforcement. He can also learn new behaviour that he has never shown himself. It is possible too using this technique to influence the actions of a large number of people at the same time.

The ability of a child to learn by observation may result in an adult unintentionally teaching him one pattern of behaviour whilst attempting to train him in another way. One argument against corporal punishment is that each time an attempt is made to train a child by hitting him he is being provided with a model for the use of successful aggression. Similarly the persistent use of sweets as a reward for a child's good behaviour may teach the advantages of bribery as a means of controlling others.

Some people have preferred the word 'modelling' rather than 'imitation' to describe the process, since the child does not copy every aspect of a 'model's' behaviour, but adapts it to his own situation. The child who is frequently beaten at home may be more likely to punch other children, but not hit them with a slipper or strap.

Bandura (1969) looked at some of the factors which make a model effective in controlling an individual's later behaviour. He reported that a filmed model could be as effective in producing changes in behaviour as a person actually performing the actions in front of the child. This clearly has implications for the effect of television, where one model can reach millions of viewers simultaneously, though whether television violence would serve as a potent model in a society which strongly disapproved of it remains to be seen. In one experiment, he asked one group of children to repeat out loud the various aspects of a model's behaviour, while a second group sat in silence. The group who made a 'verbal record' of the film were more successful in later attempts to imitate the model's behaviour. This suggests that language may serve an important function in enabling a child to store up witnessed behaviour for later performance.

By and large, experiments on modelling have demonstrated that children and adults will readily engage in aggressive behaviour following a modelling experience, provided they are in a situation where aggression is permitted. One way of demonstrating the effect of watching an aggressive film has been to assess the level of electric shock that people are willing to administer to a subject of a learning experiment as punishment for his errors. The subject is an accomplice of the experimenter and actually receives no shock. In a typical experiment, hospital attendants were tested after watching a filmed knife fight. They gave the 'learner' significantly more shocks than a group who had watched young people doing art work (Walters and Thomas, 1963).

There are relatively few experiments which demonstrate others serving as models for cooperation, though this probably reflects a research bias rather than any difficulty in obtaining positive results. In one experiment, the number of people stopping to help a girl change the wheel of her car was increased considerably by allowing the driver to encounter a quarter mile before, a girl in a similar situation but with a man helping her (Bryan and Test, 1967).

In general, the power of a model is greatest when he is perceived as possessing a high degree of competence, status and control over resources; when he has been the source of previous rewards; when he is someone to whom the individual is attached, such as parents and friends; when he is seen as being similar to the person observing him and when there are several models exhibiting similar behaviour. The observer is always influenced by the consequences of the model's actions. If the model is rewarded, he will be imitated, but not if he is punished. However, if it is clear that the observer will himself be rewarded for an action for which a model has been punished, he will quickly demonstrate that he has learnt the observed action.

Models as agents for socialization

It seems very likely that most of an individual's social role behaviour is acquired through the observation of others. It is not surprising to find that the most potent models are those with whom the individual has developed a relationship and who are similar to himself. In a situation where the individual is presented with models of high status who do not belong to his group, he may develop a certain amount of conflict that can be resolved only by rejecting the model or his own subcultural group (see B3). The middle class teacher in a school may present this situation for many of the working class children. It is important for him to be perceived as someone who accepts the subculture to which the child belongs and as willing to make a relationship with the child. If he fails to do this he

46

may be forced to rely on instrumental training, rather than modelling as the mechanism for socialization.

Many of the characteristics of a successful model are possessed by members of the children's peer group and a considerable amount can be made of this fact in actively engaging children, who have mastered a particular activity, to teach others who have not. The Russian system of education studied by Bronfenbrenner (1970) makes full use of these possibilities.

Socialization failure

We have looked at the goals of successful socialization where an individual learns the roles appropriate to a particular organization or institution. However, socialization is not always successful. For a variety of reasons the individual may find difficulty in acquiring certain roles or he may be unwilling to learn them. In either case he may be regarded as a socialization failure. I would like to examine this notion of socialization failure in relation to problems that may arise in preconditions of socialization and in later socialization. It is to be understood that most problems will arise as the result of the interaction between the child's particular set of inherited dispositions and his agents of socialization.

Failure in the preconditions for socialization

Arguing from the results of experiments on early animal development some people have thought that there are *critical periods* during an individual's life when various behaviours can be acquired and that if the opportunity is missed then it is lost for ever. It has been suggested that language has to be acquired during the first twelve years of life otherwise a language can never be learned completely (see C2). However, on a much shorter time scale, Spitz (1950) argued that unless adequate attachments were made by a child within the first nine months of his life, he would be permanently damaged in his ability to make relationships. Whilst most people regard the early years of a child's life as extremely important, it is always difficult to assess the extent to which a particular problem can be reversed. Individuals show great variability and some show a remarkable ability to withstand adverse situations. Davis (1947) reported a case of a child who was reared by a dumb mother in a dark attic until he was six who subsequently developed normal speech, made friends and did well at school. Difficulty in reversing the problem may often reflect the difficulty we have in providing the appropriate socializing experiences that an older child missed when he was younger. The varying degrees of recovery that have been made by children brought up by animals in the wild have been carefully documented by Malson (1964).

The notion of critical periods was adopted in the educational theories of Maria Montessori who felt that there were sensitive periods when a child was ready to learn something and it was the role of the teacher and parents to spot these periods and guide the child towards the appropriate learning experiences.

While the notion of critical periods may be open to doubt, it is worth looking again at the social signal systems, the formation of attachments, and the emergence of independence to see what problems may arise when their development is disrupted.

Deficiency in signal systems
Relationships depend on reciprocal behaviour where each individual adapts to the needs and wishes of the other. Where there is a defect in the social signalling system, it may be particularly difficult for a child and adult to develop a mutual relationship. Many of the features of infantile autism, which is characterized by an extreme difficulty in forming attachments, seem to relate to problems in this area. Such children are said to avoid eye contact, to have great difficulty in acquiring effective language, and it is sometimes reported that as babies they were so good that they never cried. Similar problems can occur in children who have sensory losses, particularly the deaf, who may experience considerable hardship in using

48

spoken language. Some recent trends in education for the deaf, which have discouraged the use of sign language and have attempted to limit communication to speech, have imposed severe pressures in the normal social development of deaf children (see F2). Although defects in social signalling systems may produce difficulties in making attachments, this does not mean that problems cannot be overcome, if not now, then some time in the future.

Problems in developing attachments

The literature in this area has focused on the inability of the adult agents of socialization to provide adequate care for their children. Bowlby (1953) has had considerable influence in drawing attention to the problems that children have faced through parental neglect, hospitalization, and poor quality care in some children's homes. The use of the words 'maternal deprivation' to describe the cause of these children's problems confounds a number of related difficulties. Rutter (1972) has attempted to untangle the various issues involved. We have seen how infants can become attached to individuals besides their mother and strictly speaking we should regard any problems as arising through inadequate opportunities for the formation of relationships or the disruption of relationships in general, rather than just considering attachments to the mother. The studies of large groups of children raised in children's homes have confounded the problems arising from lack of opportunities to make attachments and the lack of a stimulating environment. Thus school difficulties may relate to the lack of stimulation rather than deprivation of affection.

From our discussion, we might expect the problems arising from a failure to develop attachments to differ from those arising when attachments already formed are broken through separation. Some children are separated repeatedly from adults to whom they are beginning to get attached and it does seem that repetition of such separations finally produces a child that is unable to make relationships at all. In analysing the effect of parents separating on the development of their children Rutter found, predictably, that any problems that arose were not due to separation itself but to the degree of parental discord that preceded it.

Problems in developing independence

The development of a certain degree of independence from parents is essential if the young child is to make use of later socializing experiences. In fact, some of the responsibility for producing independent role behaviour may be taken on by a child's school or nursery school. In the development of independence, the child has to learn to function adequately in the absence of his family and to do things for himself. Clearly, both these aspects of the child's behaviour need to be encouraged during his experiences with the family. However, there are children who have such severe learning problems that they find it difficult to acquire the basic skills necessary for an independent existence. They may be unable to learn to feed themselves let alone cope with the learning demands of the daily environment of most children. Such children need frequent daily care and where the difficulties are too great to be managed at home, this may be given in special hospital units. The causes of such severe problems may be numerous, from deficiencies in the biochemical functions of the body to severe brain damage due to birth injury.

Failure in later socialization

When an individual is unable or unwilling to perform the social roles that a particular institution aims to teach him, then he can be viewed as a socialization failure. A mother complained to me about her daughter who only bathed once a week and constantly wore the same old dirty clothes. When I asked her how she felt her daughter would manage in her future life, she replied: 'Oh, she'll always make out'. The mother felt she had failed with her daughter, yet clearly, from other points of view, which regard successful outcome of family socialization as an ability to lead an independent life, she was also predicting success. The individuals who are adjusting to the role demands of future periods of their lives, may be thought to be failing in their present situations. We can only talk of socialization failure in relation to a particular institution or set of institutions. What one institution regards as a failure, another may regard as a success. A woman may leave one work organization where her employers regard her as totally incapable of filling their needs and move to a different organisation where she becomes extremely successful.

Mental illness, mental hospitals and socialization failure
Most people cope with the variety of situations in which they spend their lives with varying degrees of success. However, there are some individuals who fail to cope with most of the situations in which they live. This may either happen because they have had the misfortune to be socialized in organizations that are deficient or because they are unable to learn the roles demanded of them. Some mental illness has been said to be due to idiosyncratic socialization in the family which ill-prepares the individual for future participation in society. The strength of influence of his particular family may be so great that in reproducing the role patterns learnt in the family, he is regarded as 'mad' by the outside world. Such individuals may be socialized in special institutions or mental hospitals which make relatively simple role demands or employ drastic procedures for socializing their members. The use of major tranquilisers and electro-convulsive therapy can be viewed in this light. Societies can be pretty inventive at producing new institutions that will socialize the failures from other organizations. I am not attempting to give a total view of 'mental illness' but pointing out one perspective from which some of these problems can be viewed (see F1).

All failures of socialization may be seen from different points of view. The person in a manic state who has a feeling of exhilarating happiness may regard his life as eminently enjoyable, but his constant 'high' may be regarded by his family as requiring 'treatment'. One might think that, where possible, one should take the point of view of the individual himself as of overriding importance. In terrible disregard of this attitude, young women were placed in mental hospitals earlier in the

51

century because they made love or became pregnant before the 'appropriate' time. The practice of offering 'treatment' to homosexuals can be seen as a blatant attempt to impose the morality of one section of the community on another. This practice is sometimes defended by suggesting that homosexuals are often unhappy with their sexual orientation. However, this is not surprising in a society which regards 'gays' as suitable cases for treatment. Of course, there are people, such as psychopathic axe-men, where the direct effect of the individual on the lives of others makes their point of view the last that should be taken into account.

One goal of an organization or institution is to prepare individuals for organizations appropriate to the next stage of their lives. Hence an aim of mental hospitals is the resocialization of individuals for the roles in which they wish to engage outside the hospital (see F3). Unfortunately much of the effort within mental hospitals is directed solely towards enabling an individual to cope with the role demands of the hospital. Institutions which attempt to socialize the individual solely to meet their own demands may resemble the 'total institutions' outlined by Goffman in his book *Asylums*. The characteristics of total institutions can be described as follows:

1 Attendance is compulsory.
2 Sleep, domestic life, recreation and work all occur within the boundaries of a single limited location and according to a single plan designed to achieve the official goals of the organization.
3 The organization of the institution is incompatible with many of the basic patterns of life in society at large; particularly in the areas of family life, sexual behaviour, and work. The function of work, as an exchange of money for services, is completely altered.
4 There is a basic split between the 'inmates' and staff in authority, with no possibility of an inmate ever moving into a position of power. Social distance is maintained between staff and inmates and the patterns of communication between these groups tends to be stereotyped. The inmates are

not allowed to have knowledge of the decisions that are taken about their lives.
5 There is a systematic eradication of the old cultural values to which the inmates previously adhered.
6 The 'system' attempts to reorganize the values and attitudes of the 'inmates' towards a new picture of the world through trivial rewards and punishment by deprivation of privileges.

To the extent that a particular mental hospital or prison resembles this portrait of a 'total institution' it is unlikely to achieve success in resocializing its patients for their future lives. We can see, too, how the attempt by some families to provide this sort of framework for their children might be a recipe for madness.

Subcultural socialization and socialization failure
It is often tempting for the dominant subculture to regard the behaviour of other groups in society as examples of faulty socialization. In his book *Adolescents of East London* Peter Willmot (1966) reported that about a third of the boys in their sample were caught for petty theft during the course of their adolescence. The 'first offence' was regarded as a sign of maturity by the peer group. We can see then that stealing in this group may represent adjustment to the norms of the subculture of these boys rather than maladjustment to the norms of a different subculture. Each class group has its own pattern of illegal activities which are regarded as acceptable by their group. The middle class practice of tax evasion and the working class notion of the 'perks' of the job are two examples of such subcultural practises.

Some adult criminals, persistent offenders whose major adjustment is to prison society, can be regarded, with the long term inmates of mental hospitals, as individuals who have failed to cope with the demands of a host of organizations in 'outside' society. Many adults convicted of crime must be regarded, however, as successful products of their particular subculture who accept the problems of police and prison as a

53

calculated risk in their way of life. The youngish football crowds who chant in unison 'Your gonna get your fuckin' 'eds kicked in' must similarly be understood in terms of a pattern of socialization which has created an enjoyable enterprise out of group aggression (see B1).

The problems of social change

The vicissitudes of society pose continual problems of adjustment for its participants. In a period of industrial expansion the well socialized individual will be the good consumer. He must develop a need for individual ownership of a wide range of products; cars, washing machines, televisions, furniture. He must also be committed to the replacement of these objects as soon as they cease to be new. He will be aided in this by the well socialized manufacturer who produces articles that only have a brief effective life. As raw materials become scarce it is no longer possible to replace old articles with new ones and a fresh pattern of behaviour of consumers and manufacturers has to be developed. Social change can make socialization failures from previous successes and the new successes will be marked by their ability to adapt to the changed conditions.

The socializing professions

Mental hospitals and prisons are institutions whose aim is, in part, to resocialize people so that they can fit in once again within the institutions of their society. Certain categories of people are employed specifically to aid institutions in persuading individuals to conform to their role demands. Psychologists, social workers, psychiatrists, can be seen in this light when they attempt to encourage children and adults to adjust to their situations in their schools, families and places of work. The pattern of institutions that we have in our society is only one of a large number of possible configurations. Institutions tend to change or evolve when they no longer serve the needs of their members. When 'professionals' attempt to socialize individuals into accepting things as they are, then they are working as agents of social control.

Summary and prospect

In this chapter I have attempted to provide an additional framework with which to understand the social forces impinging on the individual. The sociological approach to the conceptions of society have to be combined with psychological research into the early development of social behaviour and the mechanisms for learning complex social roles in order to provide a total picture of the socialization process. The psychological concerns have led, too, to an appreciation of the role of the individual in shaping his own life. In the next chapter I want to explore the concept of personality in relation to the socialization process so that our attention can be focussed, further, on the development of the individual.

3
Personality and the socialization process

In the previous chapter we looked at the forces which tend to enable an individual to fit in with a particular social system. Because there are a large number of individuals who have to carry out similar social roles we have also been looking at some of the processes which make people behave in a similar way. However, I have stressed that agents and agencies of socialization are all different. Because of these differences the socialization process also serves to develop a person's individuality. We use the word personality to designate the dispositions in individuals which make them different from other people (see D3).

Traditionally sociologists have been more interested in the socialization process whereas psychologists have tended to concentrate on the factors involved in personality development. This has led to a certain amount of confusion in the literature where psychologists have tended to think that there isn't much more to the socialization process besides the development of personality and sociologists have thought there was nothing more to personality than the learning of social roles.

Freud (1930) was one of the first psychologists to use the term 'socialization'. The importance of his view does not stem necessarily from its prominence as a theory of personality at present, but in the influence it has had on other conceptions of the socialization process. It was taken up both by anthropologists and sociologists and because of the insularity of the various disciplines it persisted long after alternative models of personality development were arising in psychology. Freud then, saw the process of socialization as involving the control of the infants impulses. As a variant of the views which regard children as inherently evil, he envisaged the child as exerting a collection of antisocial impulses which if left unbridled would turn him into a raging sociopath. The needs of society were served by channelling the energy generated by these impulses in socially acceptable directions. This was achieved during the process of personality development as the child and his parents resolve the challenges presented by the various stages of his psycho–sexual development. The sex impulse which was originally aimed at the parent of the opposite sex is redirected by the resolution of the oedipal complex in a way which allows for feelings of non-sexual love towards family members and friends. The aggressive drive is redirected towards the individual himself in the form of a personal policeman, conscience or super-ego. The model of relationships that is developed in the family during this stormy period is then applied in new relationships in the wider society.

This view, then, cites the family as of over-riding importance as the socializing agency for the individual. However, this situation will only arise under a very limited set of conditions. Family socialization may suffice if all other organizations or institutions in the society require the same patterns of role behaviour that are learnt in the family and the society is in a period of social stability. Under conditions of rapid social change the parents may be poorly equipped to prepare their children for situations they have never themselves experienced. This conception really only applies, too, in those societies which have as their basic unit the nuclear family of father, mother and children. In a complex society under conditions of social change the individual needs to develop a wide range of role behaviour to meet the demands of a variety of organizations and to adapt to new situations.

Sociological views of personality

Parsons (1949) conceived of personality development, following Freud, as preparing the individual for the socialization process. The individual was made socializable and then he learnt the role behaviour appropriate to the organizations of his society. He referred to these two processes as primary and secondary socialization respectively. Yet, clearly, it is through the learning of role behaviour that individuals develop their personality. We would expect personality change to reflect in part the demands of new role behaviour that an individual has to learn throughout his life. Any view of personality development which regards it as a once and for all process runs into the problem of explaining personality change. We might say of someone 'Since he got that new job he is a changed man' as an acknowledgement of the way new role demands may alter an individual's personality.

Another view of personality, arising from sociology, has been the notion that personality is solely the set of social roles available to an individual at any one time (Brim, 1960). On this notion a personality is not something you have but only something you exhibit in relation to other people. Social roles are taught by particular organizations which demand a particular pattern of behaviour. To the extent that organizations are similar, then they will demand similar patterns of behaviour but there is no other need, on this view, to account for an individual's consistency of personality in different situations. This conception denies, too, that there is any need for a notion of personal style with which an individual acts out his social roles. However, just as an actor will bring his individual gifts to a part in a play, so each person performs his social roles with his own stamp of individuality.

Unfortunately the measurement of individual personality characteristics has run into a number of difficulties (see D4), and because of this the view that personality is a useless concept has gained a number of supporters. Most theories of personality require that we should be able to specify characteristics of an individual which show consistency in different situations and that there should be a degree of stability over time. We can illustrate the research findings by reference to the view which seeks to identify people along a series of dimensions or descriptions called traits. Psychologists have tended to be interested in traits that characterize a particular individual or social problem. Thus dependency is often studied because it is assumed that many adult problems might arise if an individual were unable to free himself from an initial close parental relationship. Aggression with its implications for delinquency, violent crime and war has been chosen equally frequently.

Stability across settings
Most experiments have found a fairly low degree of correspondence in different situations for behaviours such as dependency or aggression. An experiment by Yarrow, Cambell and Burton (1968) illustrates this point, and also the care one must take in interpreting the results of such studies. They found a slight but significant correlation in comparing the analyzed interviews with the children's mother for the behaviour at home and with the teacher for the behaviour at school (0·29 for dependency and 0·33 for aggression).

There was a slight tendency for children said to be dependent at home to also be dependent at school. Two teachers rating the behaviour of the children in nursery school obtained much closer correspondence in their independent assessments (obtaining correlations of 0·47 for dependence and 0·65 for aggression). The correspondence of the behaviour rating in school may mean that we are looking at behaviour specific to a particular situation or that the agreement is produced by the teachers' common frame of reference in answering the interviewer's questions, which neither share with the mother.

Some psychologists had hoped that better and more sensitive measuring instruments might produce more consistent findings. However, except for cognitive and intellectual measures, social and personal behaviours show a high degree of situational specificity. This had been found on such character traits as rigidity of thought, social conformity, attitudes to authority and in the willingness of an individual to cheat and deceive (Mischel, 1968). In a particularly striking experiment Mischel (1973) reported that the same child would vary in his willingness to wait for the same reward from $\frac{1}{2}$ minute to $1\frac{1}{2}$ hours, provided care was taken in preparing the child beforehand.

Stability over time

Several investigators have attempted to trace what they consider to be crucial personality variables in longitudinal studies. Kagan and Moss (1962) studied a group of boys and girls as they grew from infancy to adulthood. Their results showed that the most stable behaviour was associated with an eagerness to do well at school and at work which they termed 'orientation to achievement'. The next most stable form of behaviour could be described as conforming to a male or female sex role. Dependency showed no continuity for boys but slight continuity for girls. Similarly passivity in a girl tended to predict withdrawn behaviour for women but had much slighter predictive success for boys.

What seems to happen is that behaviour that corresponds to a particular enduring role such as sex role shows general persistence but that behaviour which conflicts with an expected role may be extinguished. Achievement orientation may persist similarly as an enduring concern of the family and social milieu into which a child is born. It is worth noting in this respect that Kagan and Moss say of their sample 'the educational and vocational characteristics of the group placed the majority of the subjects within the popular definition of middle class'. Clearly if they had chosen a different sample they might have noted a different pattern of development.

Phenotype and genotype

Where behaviour traits have failed to persist the notions of *genotype* and *phenotype* have been invoked to account for the change. Phenotype refers to the observed behaviour and genotype to the underlying structure thought to determine the behaviour. It is clear that apparently similar behaviours may occur for very different reasons and different behaviours may serve the same purpose. Thus crying behaviour in a young baby may signal bodily discomfort and in an older child may be related to fear of punishment or loss of an important object. The phenotype (crying) is served by different genotypes. From a child's point of view the dependency behaviour that achieves attention and cuddles at home may irritate the teacher and other children in school and be transformed into creative play and eagerness to help. As agents of socialization the child's parents may actually teach and encourage this shift. In this case the different phenotypes, dependency behaviour and eagerness to please, may be said to be in the service of one genotype which might be a need for affection.

The notion of a genotype as allowing a prediction of behaviour runs into several problems. If we allow a large number of genotypes we are likely to run into the same problems of continuity that is inherent in the notion of phenotype. If we only allow genotypes to include a few basic traits then the diversity of behaviour that could occur in the service of the genotype would enable us to make very few predictions.

The meaning of the research findings

The findings of these experiments seem to suggest that there is a certain slight amount of continuity in behaviour across settings and over time and this would allow a limited place for the notion of personality. However, before we conclude that most is lost for personality let us think carefully about the experimental procedure that is commonly used. You take a group of children and assess their degree of dependency, for example, in one situation. You then look at the same group of children in a different situation and find that some who were dependent are now independent and that some who were dependent are still dependent. When you average out your findings you end up with a slight tendency to be consistent in different situations. However, the results are made up of some children who are totally consistent, some who are totally inconsistent and others who are fairly consistent or fairly inconsistent. If you then picked a different characteristic, like being aggressive, or cooperative or laughing a lot, you would similarly find stability for some, instability for others and those showing stability in different characteristics might be different children. Unfortunately there is no short cut in getting to know people. When you have known someone for a long time you may discover their own particular characteristics which are stable across settings. In a psychological experiment it may be a long process to discover the characteristics of individual children which show a degree of stability, a process which may in the end be rather like getting to know a particular child. We must, however, remember that in our interaction with a particular person we provide a stable setting which changes as soon as they interact with others. (How has that miserable woman changed into such a happy optimistic lady so soon after she started going out with someone else?)

The problems of interpreting research on personality development which gives the average results for a group is equally relevant to longitudinal studies. It is amazing that so much of the research, which purports to be aimed at discovering individuality, is conducted in this way. A tendency for a trait to persist in time in a group tells us very little about what would happen to a particular individual from that group. This problem imposes severe limitations on the use of personality questionnaires in clinical psychology where one is trying to learn something about individual behaviour.

The trait theory of personality omits from its conception the notion of the individual as actively engaged in shaping his own life. In discussing the individual as a socializing agent, I introduced the idea of people as making plans and working out strategies about their future. It is the child strategist that often upsets the researcher when he weighs up the pay-offs for being aggressive in one situation and those for being comically loveable in another. In looking at the way people solve intellectual problems, some authors (e.g. Witkin, 1965) have elaborated on the notion of the cognitive style which characterizes an individual's problem solving behaviour (see D3). This approach can be usefully applied to social situations which present problems that individuals solve with a particular style of personality. We can see how dividing psychology up into subjects like cognitive psychology, perception, personal and social development, may obscure the way results from one field of enquiry can be applied by investigators in another.

Personality theory, society and subculture

Psychological theories which attempt to determine the persisting features of individual behaviour have to be specific to a particular society. This is brought out strikingly by Kagan (1973) in a recent article for *New Society* where he recants much of his previous view. In a Guatamalan village he saw: 'listless, apathetic infants, passive, quiet, timid three-year-olds; but active gay, intellectually competent eleven-year-olds'. Had he seen young children exhibiting such behaviour in American society he would have predicted a very different personality outcome for them. Until they were a year old, these children spent all their time in a dark hut with little stimulation, yet they grew up to be able to cope with a wide range of demanding problems. Kagan concluded: 'Thus it seems that the continuity of a psychological disposition does not stem from some neurological structure within the individual, separate *from external pressures*.' The course of personality development is determined largely by the way an individual is treated in his culture and the expectations of the socializing agents about age-appropriate roles. These determine the scope of his behaviour as well as the set of experiences that shape his view of the world. Just as the psychologist embarking on a longitudinal study may resemble the social historian when he comes to report it, so the psychologist working in England might resemble the anthropologist coming from Africa to study the pattern of English development. In Chapter 5 I will take a more detailed look at the variety in development in different cultures.

In the longitudinal study of Kagan and Moss we noted that the persisting personality traits could be interpreted as conforming to enduring role behaviour. Thus sex role behaviour and orientation towards achievement both persisted in the middle class group. In a social class group that could not expect any great achievement in the social system one might expect the socialization pressures of the school and subculture to considerably affect the orientation of the children. Perhaps in such a group we might find orientation to failure as a persistent trait. Similarly there may be small subgroups in society who rear their children in ways which avoid teaching sex role behaviour and we might expect such behaviour to show little continuity in these groups. Not only do theories of personality development have to be specific to a particular society but they also have to take account of subcultural influences.

The socialization process affects development as long as individuals move to different organizations and have to learn new role behaviour. Since personality development is affected by the demands of new roles we would expect it to continue throughout an individual's life.

Personal and social development through the life cycle

Much of the research and writing on the processes that shape adult personality has been influenced by a conception of development that leads to eventual stable maturity. Psychologists have borrowed this notion from the biological view of a fully grown, sexually mature organism as the last stage of the life cycle. Of course people do reach biological maturity a few years after puberty when they are fully grown and at a peak of physical strength. However the precise point at which this biological maturity is recognized as conferring adult status depends on the society in which they live. Maturity itself is a concept which varies depending on the human activity we are designating. Footballers in England may reach full maturity around the age of 26. The peak of activity for scientists will probably be at a much greater age than this. In our society the way we use the word also depends on how old we are. The seventy-year-old may be thankful that he has at last gained a mature outlook on life. Unlike the frog or butterfly, the seventy-year-old human adult knows that he has continued to develop or change throughout his life. Neugarten and Paterson (1957) found that their sample of middle-aged people perceived adulthood as four different periods: young adulthood, maturity, middle age, old age. They noted that working-class people conceived the onset of middle and old age as starting earlier than middle class people and also thought these periods started earlier for women than men.

The contexts of development and our notions of the effects of agencies of socialization can suggest ways of assessing the changes through life. Social time exerts its pressure in the form of a continued series of age-related functions. The issues of child-rearing, career structure, ageing and failing health, retirement, bereavement, as well as the new complex interrelationships to others at differing stages of the life cycle are powerful forces that shape individual experience and outlook. These reactions take place against historic time with its patterns of economic and social change which present a unique set of influences on individuals at different stages of their lives in the particular subculture of their society. Biological time continues to throw up new challenges in the ageing process and at some point unleashes its most powerful weapon which provokes the greatest change of all: death.

Younger people hold a number of misconceptions about the lives of older people in our society. When my next door neighbour of seventy-four left the woman he had been living with for thirty years to run off with another woman my conception of the lives of older people underwent a fairly radical transformation. There is something odd about reading an article by a psychologist called 'The sexless older-years: a harmful stereotype' (Rubin, 1973), when any older person could have written it from his own knowledge. Neugarten (1973) looked at the effect on personal development of menopause and reported that 85 per cent of the women she interviewed exhibited no lasting effect in their behaviour after this period. This may be because menopause in western society rarely signifies a social stage. Childbearing is generally over before this period. But she found no general change in sexual activity associated with this period either.

Many of the changes that have been assumed to be associated with ageing may be seen as a product of the social structure. We live in a society which has a limited number of employment opportunities. This determines the age when the young are allowed to enter employment and the age when the old have to leave it (see E1). It has been suggested that old age involves a process of disengagement from society (Cummings and Henry, 1961). In the sphere of employment this looks like offering someone the opportunity to resign as a polite way of saying you're fired. Planned obsolescence applies to old people too. It is clear, however, that in spheres of activity where old people are permitted to exercise a role, such as politics, they continue to make significant contributions.

As we progress through the life cycle our particular institutions of family and work gradually restrict the changes possible for the individual. The twenty-five-year-old unmarried man who has had four jobs to gain experience may be an acceptable employee but the thirty-five-year-old man who has had ten jobs to gain experience may be regarded as unstable. After the age of about forty-five it becomes increasingly difficult to change employment because of the difficulty of a person of that age being absorbed into the institutional structure of a fresh organization with its carefully preserved rituals of seniority. Stability of personal and social development can be seen as a by-product of the social structure, rather than necessarily implying an inherent age-related increase in personal rigidity.

The periods of maximum change in personal development

It has been customary to regard the early years of development as producing the most drastic changes in personality growth. In its first five years the child changes from a relatively unresponsive infant into a socialized human being with a recognizable personality style. We have noted, too, how the decrease in opportunities for many people to alter their life situation as they grow older may cause us to believe that they are incapable of changing. The enforced changes that occur for old people following retirement involve considerable curtailed social opportunities and often a drop to an income that barely covers their needs for survival. We might argue that old age involves a degree of change that is comparable to that for children. But then what about the other stages of life? The rise in importance of sexuality in the teens, the attempts at forming harmonious long-term marital relationships, the rearing of children, the changes in personal fortune produced by increased income or the onset of disabling disease may all be proposed as instigating extreme changes in personal experience and growth. One might argue that a society like ours which imposes a discontinuity in development between childhood and adulthood provokes the greatest changes when children finally enter the adult world.

Faced with these issues, I would suggest that the period of maximum change in a person's life is a matter of personal experience that will differ from individual to individual. We might even decide that the changes that occur at different ages are not even comparable. Each time of life throws up challenges that seem to be of paramount importance at that period. Having decided that development is a lifelong process it may become rather meaningless to attempt to define the most important developmental periods for all individuals.

Psychological theories of development through life

In this and the previous chapters we have seen how a psychological theory of development could be based on a knowledge of historical, biological and social contexts linked to an understanding of the social structure and socialization process. The elaboration of such a theory would be a mammoth undertaking and would even then remain specific to a particular time and society. Almost all theories of personal and social development have hooked themselves to the biological contexts of growth and have been limited to an explanation of the changes occuring from infancy to adulthood. One notable attempt to provide a framework of life time development emerged from the work of Eric Erikson (1950). He sees his theory as universally applicable but as representing only one of many possible ways of regarding the course of human development. The individual is conceived as being faced with a succession of issues or problems that he must resolve with the others around him in the context of the maturation and ageing processes. Erikson has developed his theory under influences of the Freudian 'psychoanalytic' approach to development and the theory is expressed in the terms of that approach. Whilst Freud viewed the main 'pacer' of development as residing inside the child in the form of *psychosexual* preoccupations, Erikson sees the child's development as largely influenced by social forces; hence his theory is said to describe *psychosocial* stages.

The issue that is associated with a particular stage of life is viewed as optimally solved during a particular period. If the child or adult fails to resolve the problem at the most appropriate time he can still achieve success later on in his life, though this is likely to become increasingly difficult with passing time. Unfortunately the reverse process can also occur. A child who has mastered the first psychosocial stage, for example, and has developed a basic trust in others may have his confidence undermined by adverse experiences later. We can view the progression through these stages as a game of psychic snakes and ladders. In describing Erikson's view I have tried to avoid his jargon, and hope that the resulting scheme still bears a fairly close relationship to his intentions.

(1) *Trust vs. mistrust* (age up to one year). During the first year of the child's life he is very heavily dependent on the person taking care of him. He may either learn that his parent provides a stable source of affection on which he can rely or remain in a state of uncertainty about whether his basic needs will be met.

(2) *Autonomy vs. shame and doubt* (second and third year). Having developed a strong attachment to adults on whom he can rely, the child is enabled to detach from them and begin to develop an ability for doing things for himself. The central issue at this stage is the building of the child's confidence in himself as being capable of an independent existence.

(3) *Initiative vs. guilt* (fourth and fifth year). During this period the child is said to be struggling with the strong feelings of the oedipal conflict (see p. 22) and also developing new ways of thinking about and exploring his environment. If his 'natural' sexual and intellectual curiosity is thwarted he may be left with a sense of guilt; a feeling that his natural self is bad.

(4) *Industry vs. inferiority*. During the period from six to eleven years the child begins to indulge in settled activities through which he may learn the skills of his culture. If he compares himself unfavourably with other children or is made to feel inadequate by others he will develop feelings of inferiority which will interfere with the development of his skills.

(5) *Identity vs. role confusion*. The twelve- to eighteen-year-old child is said to experience a series of challenges involving his attitudes to himself, to his friends, to members of the opposite sex and to a future career. To the extent that others

around him enable the resolution of these issues he will develop a strong feeling of personal identity.

(6) *Intimacy vs. isolation.* The theme for the young adult is seen as centreing around the building of lasting and deep relationships usually with another of the opposite sex. It is in this period that the individual may build a deep strong commitment to his own family.

(7) *Generativity vs. self-absorption.* The choice involved in the middle years of life involves looking outward towards society and making a valuable contribution or remaining totally concerned with one's own physical and material comforts.

(8) *Integrity vs. despair.* The central problem for the older person is seen as the accomplishment of a self-view which involves regarding one's life as a worthwhile progression; regret over missed opportunities and mistakes leads to a sense of despair over one's inability to start again.

The reader can consider whether these stages apply universally both for individuals in different societies and for different individuals in different sub-cultures of the same society. Clearly there is an implied view that certain patterns of growth are healthy whereas others involve a developmental failure. The hermit who chooses to spend his time in isolation from the world is to be judged as never passing stage 5. Similarly we might see the emergence of the fourth stage (industry vs. inferiority) only in cultures which stressed competition and penalized children because they did not develop certain skills at a particular stage in their lives.

The search for universals

Throughout the literature there is a consistent reference to the universal features of mankind and society. We have seen how so many influences combine to produce development that it depends heavily on the context in which it occurs. In our look at the literature in social history, across cultures and within different subcultures, we will be confronted with evidence which may enable us to determine the extent of a universal pattern of development and we will return to this theme in the last chapter.

Robin Fox, an anthropologist, in his book on *Kinship and Marriage* (1967) states in his preface that he is primarily interested in the question 'What is man?' In examining the various patterns of family structure in different societies he concludes that the basic universal unit involves mother and child. However, we can see that this notion of a basic unit is by no means essential. Children *can* be brought up by people other than their parents. We can easily imagine societies, particularly where cows provide a substitute for breast milk, where all children are reared by adults other than their mothers.

There is another misconception common in the psychological literature that behaviour that can be shown to be in part biologically determined cannot also be specific to a particular culture (see C1). It has been found, for example, that convicted criminals have a higher incidence of an inherited sex-chromosomal abnormality. Development involves a constant interaction between social and inherited influences. It is quite possible to imagine that one set of factors tends to create criminals out of these individuals whilst in a different society they might take on entirely different roles. The apparent lack of a clear-cut determination of so many individual characteristics can be viewed with disappointment or with a sense of optimism that individual malleability allows for possibilities of worthwhile social change.

We may find that a particular psychological relationship or apparent developmental stage that occurs in our society does not occur under different conditions. Of course, this does not then make it an uninteresting subject for study. The influences of our society are the ones which most affect our lives and as we understand them we gain a greater capacity to determine our future.

71

4
Past, present and future

We have looked at some of the ways of describing societies and at the processes by which an individual adjusts to his society and develops his individuality. We have seen how the psychologist, struggling to develop a theory of personality, may come to resemble the anthropologist looking at the processes shaping a cultural group. He may also resemble a social historian, studying the processes at work at one point in time in the development of his society. The psychology of personality development has often been based on the hopeful assumption that man does not change, yet it is clear that the socialization process which helps to determine our lives is constantly altered by changing historical influences.

The individual grows up in the context of a constant interaction with the changing institutions of his society. This pattern of institutions sets a limit on his personal and social opportunities which create the experiences that shape his life. We can considerably enhance our understanding of these limits by studying the way the institutions of our society have emerged historically and the forces that have combined to produce the changes. An appreciation of the way social institutions have arisen through an interplay of historical forces might also enable us to assess whether these institutions fulfil our present needs.

The essential argument of this book has been that individuals are moulded by their experiences; different experiences produce different people. In his book *The Changing Nature of Man*, J. H. Van den Berg (1961) suggested the term 'historical psychology' to define the study of the way people have changed as a result of altering historical conditions. In his view, historical psychology involves 'comparing the past and present with the object of finding in what ways modern man differs from man in previous generations. It also seeks the reasons and the causes of the changes'.

Historical psychology is not to be confused with *histories of psychology* which attempt to trace the development of the science of psychology with a view to outlining a progression of discoveries about people. Histories of psychology emphasize the development of psychology and the stability of people. Anderson (1956) wrote an article called 'Child development: An historical perspective', in which he outlined the series of discoveries that have been made about the child as a biological system over the last hundred years. Yet, in the same period children have changed tremendously. A constantly changing environment means that 'man arrives at every age of life as a novice' (Berg, 1961), and also that at each period of history the psychologist is presented with a new subject for study.

Not only do psychologists attempt to study a constantly changing subject matter, but what they 'discover' may also be influential in producing changes. Thus, a view that a child has 'naturally' aggressive impulses that need to be expressed and that will disappear in the normal course of development may lead parents to practise permissiveness towards aggression that the child may interpret as active encouragement. A generation of more aggressive adults might be produced in part by the influence of a previous generation of permissive psychologists. It is this sort of realization which recently led Dr Spock of 'baby care' fame to backtrack on some of his earlier views.

In looking at the changing patterns of socialization, we have to make some decision about how far back into history to delve. I cannot hope to trace all the changes in all the societies of the world since the beginning of man. What I will try to do is to examine some of the influences on the changing institutions of family, school and work and the changing preoccupations of various stages in the life cycle as they have emerged in recent history.

From past to present

Three hundred years ago, childhood did not exist in European countries for the vast majority of the population. After a relatively short period of dependent infancy, children moved directly into adult society. They did the same work, played the same games and laughed at the same jokes. At a similar period, there were very few old people as we think of them today. People were very old at fifty and most could not expect to reach that age. There were few schools and the mass of the population were illiterate. The lives of the working people were ruthlessly controlled by the landed gentry and the 'merchant princes' of the cities. There was little notion of privacy; the idea of the nuclear family as a separate unit, catering to the emotional needs of parents and children, did not exist. Nobody talked about the problems of the relationship between children and adults, because the groups were not divided. Nobody needed vocational guidance, because job allocation was virtually determined by birth.

These last three hundred years have seen the growth of schools and the development of the nuclear family, the emergence of the role of housewife and the notions of childhood, adolescence and now youth (Keniston, 1968) as stages of the life cycle. Associated with these stages are a host of experts specializing in the treatment of childhood and adolescent problems and diseases. Together with the mass media, they have created a series of 'myths' about human development which are very difficult to separate from the truth.

In a carefully documented book, Philip Aries has traced the

emergence of childhood and its association with the growth of schooling and the changing patterns of family life. He concluded that: 'The stages of individual development recognized by cultural convention depend on the existence of specific social institutions. Childhood emerged with the introduction of the modern school and the bourgeois family.' (Aries, 1962)

Since the publication of Aries' book, there has been renewed interest in the changing patterns of development. However, 'blindness to the past' is still a fairly prevalent disorder among psychologists. In the concluding paragraph of her book *Males and Females*, Corrinne Hutt (1972) adduced a government report in support of her thesis about differences between men and women: 'The research team found that ... a range of patterns will be needed – among them the old *traditional* pattern of the housewife at home – to match the circumstances and personalities of different married couples.' The housewife is a tradition that barely extends back over the last hundred years. Not only do the myths of universal childhood and adolescence, home and family, need exploding but they also need explaining. It may seem surprising, in view of the ease with which we can obtain evidence to the contrary, how many people presume that the pattern of life of their group in society during their life time must apply for other groups, at other times, or in other societies. Elizabeth Janeway devoted most of her book, *Man's World, Women's Place* to an attempt to explain the myth that woman's place has been at the 'hearth' for any but a small proportion of women for a relatively short period of history.

In looking in more detail at the changes in institutions, I propose to consider first some of the background conditions that have prompted them to change. The Industrial Revolution transformed society. It was associated with tremendous changes in population structure and was the major impetus in reorganizing education and family life. Ivan Illich has concentrated a large part of his considerable energy on attempting to protect the under-developed nations from a wholesale adoption of institutions thrown up by the historic forces of the

75

industrialized nations. He had this to say of childhood: 'Since most people live outside industrial cities, most people today do not experience childhood ... only with the advent of the industrial society did the mass production of childhood become feasible and come within the reach of the masses.' (Illich, 1972)

The background to social change

It has been argued that the greatest force for social change that ever occurred was the discovery of crop cultivation and the domestication of animals, which enabled groups of men and women to change their way of life from a nomadic existence in search of sources of food to a life which permitted large groups to settle in a permanent home base. In living and co-operating together these groups were able to develop complex rules and rituals to regulate their interactions (Dubos, 1972). Agricultural improvements and the possibilities of external trade reduced the necessity for the vast majority of the population to involve themselves in agriculture. Developing technology, the use of the coal as a source of fuel, and the increase in international trade, provided the powerful with a tremendous opportunity to increase their wealth. These new opportunities also created a chance for an increasing group of individuals to break away from the limitations of inherited wealth to an intermediate position between the aristocracy and the poor; they formed the new middle classes.

From agriculture to industry

At the turn of the eighteenth century in England most of the population still lived in the country; London was already a town of half a million people but no other town had a population that exceeded 50,000. The vast majority of urban dwellers lived in abject poverty. However, the life on the land was not much easier. Changes in the laws of land tenureship obliged many to give up eking out an existence using their allotments and the commons, and forced them into the city slums where they shared their 'hovels' with their animals and made a communal toilet of the street (Plumb, 1950).

The agricultural life had been one of full employment for every member of the family. Children were an asset because they helped on the land. Women, when they were not actually confined by the brief period needed for the birth of their children, worked a full day in the fields often accompanied by the youngest child that was still being breast fed. The early period of industrialization saw the development of domestic industries. The working people extended their home crafts, such as those involved in making clothes, to meet the demands of the great manufacturers. The period of domestic industry was still one of full employment in which parents exploited their children to obtain increased production. Little girls were chained to the spinning wheel from morning until night (Pinchbeck, 1969).

Mechanization gradually reduced the need for home industries and forced more and more adults out of their homes and into factories. There was clearly a tremendous variation in the demand for labour in various parts of the country, but improved technology and the rapid rise in the size of population in the nineteenth century meant that there were far more people than jobs. In some places this produced a continued demand for cheaper female labour at the expense of the men, and in others a sudden drop of the value of women to the economics of the home and a consequent increase in the marriage age. Industry became a competing ground for jobs between men, women and children which was partly resolved by male domination of the emerging unions (Rowbotham, 1973). It is difficult from the perspective of the twentieth century to evaluate to what extent progressive legislation that protected children from the harsh working conditions of the factory and pit was a response to the reduced demand for labour by the factory and pit owners. However, the large numbers of children that were left roaming the streets of Victorian England was certainly a potent force in the development of universal education that probably far outweighed the effect of the voices of radical educationalists.

The separation of members of the family from a contribution to home economics had first extended from the nobility to the middle classes where business men and the new breed of professionals went away from home to their place of work. It became part of the middle class status for the woman to be relegated to a position of leisure at home. Boys were sent away to the 'public' schools and girls were expected to acquire 'accomplishments' at home. The labour demands of industry began to extend this process into working class homes.

The effect of population changes

Industrialization has been paralleled in every country in the world by a rapid increase in population. The massive growth in population of England only began during the nineteenth century. From 5 million inhabitants in 1700, there were 11 million in 1800 but by 1900 there were 39 million. The population of this country has now levelled off at about 56 million. The population increase created problems of distribution of goods and instigated the formation of large bureaucratic organizations to regulate distribution, control taxation, and crime. The mass of urban poor chosen for description by early sociologists added impetus to the generation of welfare organizations, which have grown at an accelerating rate since the end of the nineteenth century.

Infant survival. It has been estimated that, in order for the population to replace itself at the present time we have to average about $2\frac{1}{2}$ births per family. The mortality rate in the middle of the seventeenth century was about 75 per cent before the age of five years (Sangster, 1963). In order just to maintain the population, families would have to average at least ten children. The estimates of the infant mortality rate taken from the cities probably overestimate the average rate in the country as a whole. However, we can see how population growth at a particularly high rate was not feasible in the country until the infant mortality rate dropped. In 1870, 15 per cent of children were dead by the end of their first year, but in 1970 only 2 per cent of children failed to survive this period.

In discussing the notion of children as socializing agents, I mentioned that they had not always exerted the influence that they do today. In a situation where families expected most of their offspring to die, the infant was not to be taken too seriously until he had proved that he was likely to survive. The main concerns of parents, when they were concerned, would have been purely for his physical well being. Montaigne had commented on his offspring: 'I have lost two of my children in infancy with regret but without grief'. The differing survival rates in poor and better off families was an important factor in forming subcultural differences in attitudes to child-rearing. Whereas 83 per cent of middle class children were surviving beyond the age of five by 1871, the figure for the population as a whole was only 63 per cent. We are told today about the greater childcentredness of the middle classes, and this may be traced back, in part, to the influence of these simple statistics.

Child survival interacted in an interesting way with the ideas of great philosophers of previous periods. Rousseau's educational theories suggested delaying any real instruction until after puberty, the time of the child's 'second birth'. He must have been influenced by the irrelevance to educators of the 'first birth' of many children, for he gave them the advice: 'of all children that are born, scarcely one half reach adolescence, and it is very likely that your pupil will not live to be a man'.

Perhaps we can trace our society's preoccupation with age to the drop in infant mortality. It was not until 1836 that parliament brought in the birth registration act.

Some of the earliest children's literature was aimed at preparing children for an early grave. In a book written for parents to read aloud to their children, Whitaker (1693) wrote: 'This may be the last month, or week, or day that you have to live ... go into the shops, and see if there be no coffins your size: go into the churchyard and see if there be no graves your length'.

Family size. There has been a dramatic decrease in family size associated with increasing child survival rates. 61 per cent of women married in 1870 had more than four children, whereas of those married in 1925 only 4 per cent had five or more. The change from a common situation of families having fourteen or fifteen children, of whom only a couple outlived their parents, to a small number that survived and could become known intimately, provided further potential for the development of family life.

Development of contraception. Contraception became an issue in the nineteenth century and was advocated for two reasons. One group of people thought that the working classes should be controlled before they swamped the nation. Another group saw effective contraception as at last allowing men and women the right to sexual expression without the fear of unwanted children.

The use of contraceptives has meant that in this century an increasing number of families can choose the time they want to have children. The development of the 'pill', IUD, and the practice of vasectomy have now removed many of the disadvantages of mechanical methods.

Class differences in family size have developed over the years with size of family being related to financial situation for the middle and upper classes, but with large families still persisting among the poorest group in the population. These differences may be related, historically, to the fact that the pressure for contraception was a middle class movement, half of which was actually aimed at the repression of the working classes.

Increased longevity. Death cannot of course only be associated with the first stage of life. The overall survival rates have also changed. In 1840 men lived an average of forty years and women forty-two years. In 1900 these figures had risen to 44 and 48 years respectively, but in the projected figures for children born in 1970 the average life expectancy is 69 years for men and 75 years for women (Sillitoe, 1970). At last men can on the average be expected to outlive the retirement age! Like all projections into the future there may well be significant errors of calculation; new diseases or new cures might radically alter the picture. The figures confound, too, the infant mortality rate with the life expectancy, so that someone who survived age five in 1840 could have expected to live rather longer than forty years; probably to around fifty-five. The large number of people over retirement age in the present population (13 per cent) was a phenomenon that hardly existed a hundred years ago. Longevity has invented retirement and the institutions, problems and possibilities, that are associated with it.

Improvement in obstetric techniques have almost eradicated the death of women in childbirth. At the turn of the century one in fifteen women died whilst giving birth to their first child and one in thirty in giving birth to the second. The vagaries of death in previous times meant that children commonly lost one or other or both parents, and step-parents were far more common. The census of 1901 reported that one woman in eight over the age of twenty was a widow. It has been suggested that death obviated the necessity for the higher divorce rates of the present day!

The explanation of population changes
The most important single factor in reducing infant mortality and increasing longevity seems to have been the improvement in the diet of the population. This seems to have applied both to the poor and, to an admittedly lesser extent, to the rich, until there was an increased awareness of the importance of correct nutrition. Radical innovations in sanitation in the cities controlled disease and reduced the possibility of epidemics. The appalling working conditions in factories accounted for a fairly large number of deaths in the eighteenth and nineteenth centuries.

Although medicine has taken a fair amount of credit for prolonging life, many of the apparently great medical conquests are illusory.

81

Tuberculosis, a great killer at the beginning of the nine-teenth century, had virtually disappeared before the development of antibiotics. Cholera, dysentery and typhoid had similarly peaked and dwindled outside medical control. 90 per cent of the decline in death rate between 1860 and 1965 for children under fifteen from scarlet fever, diphtheria, whooping-cough and measles had occurred before wide-spread immunization ... The study of the evolution of disease provides evidence that during the last century doctors have affected such patterns no more profoundly than did priests during earlier times. (Illich, 1975)

The preoccupations of medicine have also contributed further to one of the most startling differences between life now and in previous times. Death has been nudged and then forced into the background. Increasingly the old as well as the sick die in hospitals after a tremendous effort to prolong their lives by a few hours. Death has ceased to be an integral part of our lives.

The emerging stages of life

The development of childhood took place against a back-ground of industrialization and changing population trends which produced a new focus on family and children. These trends accelerated the changes that were being urged on the nobility by the moralists of the sixteenth century. If the adult population was to be saved then the innocence of their children had to be preserved, and this could only be achieved by their removal from the corrupting influence of certain sections of adult society. The church, industrialization, the ideas of influential philosophers, population changes, develop-ment of schools, the ideal of family life and the need for conscription into the army were some of influences which broke up the uniform society of the Middle Ages into the various age related stages of child, adolescent and adult. We shall see that some of the presumed characteristics of these stages were more real than others. Some stemmed from the minds of the theorists who described them, whilst others developed through the pressures of the institutions by which they were maintained. As the stages of life of 'the child', 'the adolescent' and 'the youth' have been separated from the concept of the mature adult, the very separation has paradoxically made us more ignorant of the nature of the people designated by these stages. We noted earlier how in our age-segregated society the young have a similar problem in discovering the lives of the old (p. 65).

The birth of childhood

Aries (1962) traced the converging focus on childhood from the Middle Ages to the present day by analysing the changes in depicting children and their families in art, in the development of special children's clothing, and through the games, toys, books and entertainments that characterized particular age groups.

Prior to the sixteenth century children were depicted in art as small adults and there were few portraits of family groups. Although the existence of children in Stuart times was only possible in the context of a family (Laslett, 1965) they grew up among an extended group of adults with whom they could interact. The idea of the small family was not important enough to merit pictorial recording or any place of prominence in the literature of the period.

The common practice of apprenticing children to other households meant that children frequently left their own homes by the age of seven to enter other families. Apprenticeship occurred either in the homes or hovels of other labourers, or in the big houses of the nobility or wealthy traders. These 'big houses' might contain thirty or forty people, comprising servants, apprentices, bailiffs and managers, clerks and clerics as well as a changing population of visitors and hangers on. About 20 per cent of the population lived in these houses in the seventeenth century (Janeway, 1972). Unlike houses of today, the rooms of these dwellings were interconnected. Servants, artisans and nobility passed through each others rooms with little possibility of privacy or concealment of the intimate lives of adults from children. The cramped conditions of the hovels had been a situation in which young children became aware of the facts of life at a very early age; sex, anger, violence and death as a not infrequent bed companion gave them a clear picture of the world they were to inherit.

Before the seventeenth century, as soon as children were out of the 'girlish' baby clothes, they wore smaller versions of adult dress. At about 1600 various signs of childhood became apparent. The boys of the nobility began to be dressed differently to their parents; often in the clothes of the adult labouring classes. However even by the end of the seventeenth century girls went straight from swaddling clothes into adult female dress. An examination of this evidence, taken together with the neglect of education for girls and their continued forced marriage at a very early age, suggests that childhood did not apply to women until long after it had been recognized for men (Firestone, 1972).

Games and entertainments used to be enjoyed by everybody. Dancing was a universal pastime of the sixteenth century in which even religious orders participated:

On summer days the prioress used to take the community for a walk a good way from the Abbey, when often the monks would come and dance with these nuns as naturally as one would do something nobody would dream of criticising. (Quoted in Aries, 1962)

By 1600 the first childrens' toys appeared though these were expected to be discarded by the age of three or four. Specific games were adopted for children by 1700 and these tended to imitate adult entertainment of previous generations.

At a corresponding period, under the influence of the church moralists, the boys of the nobility were sent away to school to escape the corrupting influence of the servants. Family portraits began to increase in popularity and the seventeenth century witnessed some of the first sentimental writing about children. They began to develop as playthings for adults, who were amused by their childlike habits and speech. The virtues of family life began to be extolled, and this created a certain amount of conflict between the educationalists and the advocates of the family as the source of all moral and academic training. However, there is no doubt that by the eighteenth century the family, the child and the school had arrived. They were to gain in importance continually up until the present day.

Infantile sexuality. Heroard, who recorded the details of Louis XIII's childhood as his physician at the beginning of the seventeenth century, mentions the frequency with which sexual comments were made to the child: 'The Queen touching his penis said "Son I am holding your spout"'. The young prince had a firm grasp of the function of his sexual organs by the age of four: 'The court were amused to see his first erections; waking up ... he exclaimed: "My cock is like a drawbridge; see how it goes up and down"'. The prince was expected to develop modesty when he was ten, but the idea of early childhood modesty did not emerge until much later. It seems that Freud rediscovered the infantile sexuality of the middle classes at the beginning of the twentieth century, much to their horror.

Ryerson (1961) traced the medical advice on childrearing from 1550 to 1900. Prior to the eighteenth century parents were enjoined to be permissive about weaning, toilet training and expressions of sexuality. The nineteenth century witnessed a change in attitude with the introduction of feeding schedules, early toilet training and severe restraint on infantile sexual interest. This severe approach reached a peak in about 1920 when masturbation was to be curbed by sewing the child's sleeves over his hands and tying his legs down. The new permissiveness only began to emerge in the 1930s (Wolfenstein, 1953).

The appearance of indications of childhood by different styles of dress, toys and games preceded any appreciation of differences between the minds of adults and children. At the end of the sixteenth century Montaigne suggested to a friend who was expecting the birth of her child, 'if you want to do something useful confront the child with philosophical discourses ... from the moment it is weaned ... the child will be able to stand philosophical discourses much better than an attempt to teach it to write and to read; this had better wait a little'.

A hundred years later in 1693 John Locke was advocating the use of reason: 'they understand it as early as they do language; and if I misobserve not, they like to be treated as rational creatures'. Although this notion fits in with the liberal conception of twentieth century childrearing, it still maintains that there is no essential difference between the understanding of children and adults. It was left to Rousseau to formulate these differences clearly: 'The child is a child, not an adult; you are the adult ... there should be reasonableness between adults; use force when dealing with the child.' Rousseau had even more to say on the distinction: 'what the child should know is that it is weak and that you, the adult, are strong; and from this difference it follows that it is under your authority. That is what the child should know, that is what it ought to learn, that is what it must feel.' (*Emile*, 1762)

Until the child was fifteen Rousseau believed that education consisted solely in shielding 'the heart from vice and the mind from error'. He felt that the child in his development paralleled the stages of animal living. The first five years were the animal stage; the child learnt to adapt physically to his surroundings and was guided by pleasure and pain. Between the ages of five and twelve he entered the stage of the simple savage; he was guided by his senses, interested in sports but lacked reasoning ability or moral considerations. The period of twelve to fifteen saw the emergence of curiosity, and a renewal of energy and increase in strength. At fifteen the child was reborn, his sex drive emerged and he was to become the recipient of his education.

With our acceptance of the idea of a long period of childhood in the present day it is difficult to place ourselves in the situation of observers of the eighteenth century who were noticing it for the first time. Because children and adults were, by and large, treated in a similar way, it just never occurred to them that they were different. Victor Hugo claimed that 'Columbus only discovered America, I discovered childhood.' However, childhood had to be invented before it could be discovered. It was invented by the gradually increasing distinction between the young and the old. This does not mean that real discoveries have not been made about the way the modes of thought of children change as they get older (see C2). What is open to question is whether these differences between groups of people in any way necessitated the separation of one group from the other. People had managed in the society of the Middle Ages. If adults had not really known how to relate children at that time, we might have seen the separation of children from adult company at a much earlier period in history.

The transition from childhood to adulthood

When the child was fifteen years old Rousseau spoke of a 'moment of crisis' when the individual became psychically mature. Although he had separated the notions of childhood and adulthood he did not envisage a long period of transition during which the individual was half man and half child. The elaboration of this period did not occur for more than a hundred years after Rousseau described the development of Emile. It is interesting that even then Rousseau had felt that the development of girls was relatively unimportant. It is quite remarkable that the stereotypes about children have changed quite dramatically, yet the view of women as intuitive, emotional creatures who are not suited to the rigours of high level intellectual pursuits has persisted with little alteration over hundreds of years.

In 1859 Charles Darwin published *The Origin of the Species* where he described the way the human species had evolved by means of natural selection. His ideas about the changes that occurred in various species were adapted into theories about the course of human development and also used to describe the forces producing social change. G. Stanley Hall, following some of the earlier ideas of Rousseau, adopted such a theory of development in which the human infant was said to live through the stages of evolution from a fish in the womb to a crawling quadruped until finally he emerged as a human adult. This process was termed recapitulation. At puberty the child began trying to break loose from the 'ancient moorings' of his primitive ancestry and this battle with the past gave rise to an adolescent period of 'storm and stress'. The stage began at twelve and had an undefined finishing point in adulthood.

The emergence of the literature on adolescence was remarkably sudden. Aristotle had given a brief description of tempestuous, sexually energized youth two thousand years previously, and in 1904 Hall produced a two volume work of nine hundred pages. These adolescents showed an instability of attitudes, a rejection of adult values, a lack of realism and a preference for peer group relationship. They were at the mercy of sexual temptation and were warned against the dangers of wearing 'tight underpants' and trousers with loose pockets. They were encouraged to seek cool temperatures lest the heat of their blood should unleash their sexual appetites.

What seems to have happened is that a view of the child as passing through evolutionary stages caused Hall to develop a theory in which children passed through a universal stage of adolescence. The 'storm and stress' which could be observed in some young people was assumed to be occurring in all of them. Hall was not very concerned with finding a representative sample of the population on which to base his observations and develop his theory. His theory had to be true, even though he was aware that the facts did not always fit it. He noticed that American adolescents all seemed 'precocious' and were 'leaping rather than growing into maturity'.

We have seen a move in psychology in recent times away from the prominence of theory as representing an ideal form of behaviour towards theories that are based on careful observation of meticulously chosen samples (see C1). However, the conception of the ideal adolescent has proved to be one of the most popular stages of life ever invented. Possibly the greatest output in articles and books in developmental psychology concern this period. 'Our society has passed from a period which was ignorant of adolescence to a period in which adolescence is the favourite age. We now want to come to it early and linger in it as long as possible.' (Aries, 1962)

One possibility is that at the turn of this century, in the groups that psychologists most frequently wrote about, many more children did display the 'typical' adolescent period than they do today. In analysing the research for the period 1890–1940, F. Musgrove (1967) found that most research studies showed qualified support for a break between the attitudes of children and their parents. However after the 1950s the reverse seems to have been true, and this has led Margaret Mead to the conclusion that the 'breech between adolescents and parents, so characteristic of American middle class culture a generation ago has narrowed'. We can note her unashamed use of the phrase 'middle class culture'. So often the universal prescriptions of psychologists turn out to refer, on closer examination, to the dominant group in society. In their 1955 article, 'The myth of adolescent culture', Elkin and Westley again looked at a 'middle class' group. They found no evidence for 'storm and stress' in their sample. By the age of fourteen or fifteen these adolescents had already internalized the ideals and values of surrounding adult society in terms of career and marriage goals. There was no sign of a rejection of adult values or participation in a youth culture. Similar results have been reported for a working class group, but then perhaps they never used to have a typical 'middle class' adolescence anyway.

In the 1950s the American universities were said to be disturbed because their students were too quiet; they were unadventurous and unquestioning. On the other hand in England in the 'fifties attention became focused on the mods and rockers, delinquent gangs that fought 'on the beaches' around the English coast. It is evident, however, that the tendency of some young people to engage in novel, destructive or revolutionary behaviour, does not then create a new developmental stage of the working class adolescent.

Adolescent characteristics

The fact that adolescents cannot be uniformly characterized as a rebellious group undergoing emotional turmoil who reject the values of their elders does not mean that there are no characteristics of this period. Some characteristics do result from the biological changes that occur at puberty, whilst others result from the institutions of school that have been given the task of teaching and containing an ever older yet earlier maturing group. However the effect that the rapid increase in sex drive has on the individual is very largely dependent on how it is treated by others. The sexual ignorance which has produced the necessity for sex education in schools may be a relatively new occurrence for most children.

In Victorian England sexual relationships were common at a very early age for the majority of the population, despite the reputation for stern morality amongst the middle classes. In recent times we have seen a re-emergence of tolerance towards masturbation and an availability of contraceptives to younger people. We have not, as a society, reached the stage where the 'establishment' smiles on the free expression of sexuality among the young, as soon as they feel the need, though some groups of young people are sufficiently insulated from these values not to be influenced by them.

Puberty is also followed by a rapid increase in size and strength. Many children reach adult size and strength before they leave school. They are physically and intellectually fitted to joining the adult world of work whilst still being obliged to sit at desks. The school child who feels himself to be an adult may provide a particularly strong challenge to a teacher or parent who refuses to grant him adult status.

The period after puberty certainly is related to an increase in sexual interest and practice and in growth and strength.

The institution of school, particularly with the raising of the school leaving age to sixteen, has made adolescence a period of enforced uncertainty about working life. Although a large number of children follow the careers of their parents, a sizeable proportion are left in a state of uncertainty until they have tried out their first jobs. This period of enforced 'identity confusion', as Erikson has called it, is often prolonged in the sizeable minority of young people who go on to further education.

The appearance of youth

The 'sixties and 'seventies have witnessed a whole series of youthful revolt around the world. Perhaps the most note-worthy in their discovery of 'student power' were the students of Paris who took to the streets with a fair measure of worker support in an attempt to change what they regarded as an oppressive regime. The discovery of student power reverberated into the universities around the world and has been associated, predictably, with yet another new stage of life: Youth.

Kenneth Keniston (1968) identified an age stratum of American society brought up in the postwar affluence who were economically secure but with an uncertain thermonuclear future. He compared the 6·4 per cent of young Americans who completed high school in 1900 with the 80 per cent who did so in 1970; the 238,000 college students at the beginning of the century with the 7,000,000 who attended college seventy years later. These were rated by a 1970 Gallup Poll as America's major social problem. Keniston resisted the temptation to regard the views of this group as those of adolescents who just couldn't grow up. He saw them as often being impelled by an accurate analysis of the perils and injustices of the world and as resisting the adoption of what other sections of the community regarded as mature adult status. Without providing any evidence, he insists that the 'youth' are not limited to one class group and advocates that they be accepted as a new 'psychological stage'.

We have seen in discussing the contexts of development

how each age stratum of society is shaped by particular individual historic forces which affect no other group. To that extent we can regard every age stratum as a new psychological stage, yet I am convinced that there is little point in doing so. The young who are not yet forced into a socializing pattern by their weekly pay packet, will always be a potential focus for political and social change.

Before they are fully affected by the socializing pressures of the institutions of their society, young people are in a unique position to challenge the validity of these organizations. Neither have they yet succumbed to the age pressures of passing life time which greet us with the nagging concern about ensuring our own individual comfort within an urban society. This is epitomized by the advertisement of the forty-year-old who ruefully expresses his fears about the inadequacy of his retirement pension. The situation where young people challenge the institutions of their society does not arise because they are at a particular age but because our social structure effectively gives maximum political freedom to them. Keniston asks: 'How should one describe a twenty-four-year-old who has yet to settle his relationship with the existing society, a vocation, his social role and life style'. 'A person'? No a 'youth'! It is amazing how people feel they have explained something when they have given it a label.

Childhood and adulthood

One fact that many writers have failed to notice is that a development of a notion of childhood also involves a change in the view of adulthood. The homogeneous culture of the Middle Ages might have appeared far more childlike than the culture of today. As groups were gradually divided up into children, adolescents and adults the characteristics of each group of individuals changed. A distance was created between adults and children which led to a decrease in understanding of the lives of each group.

In all societies which adhere to a rigid distinction between children and adults the capabilities and knowledge of the children are consistently underestimated and those of adults overestimated both by themselves, and by their children (Goodman, 1964). Several writers have commented on the lack of real intellectual precocity in recent times compared to some of the great musicians and philosophers of previous periods (e.g. Berg, 1961). In attempting to bridge this gap between adults and children we have evolved professional experts on childhood. One might imagine that a further advance in reducing the gulf might ensue from the recruitment of children as experts on adult behaviour!

If we regard the 'gap' between adults and children as a problem then we need to think of ways in which any division can be breached so that children can be permitted to know more about adult life and adults can once more be allowed to enter the world of childhood. The experts who see adolescent rebellion as a necessary stage of growth are attempting to make a universal virtue out of a limited truth. In a situation where adults resist the granting of full adult independence to their children it is not surprising that some children fight to achieve it.

The fourteen-year-old of today is biologically advanced by $2\frac{1}{2}$ years over his age-mate of a hundred years ago. His counterpart of that time was usually integrated fully into adult life and often had some measure of choice over where he resided. Admission to the army was the institutional counterpart for adolescence, just as the school and family aided the development of childhood. In the last century a boy could be a lieutenant in the French army at fourteen. In these contexts it is not surprising that adolescent runaways have become an increasing problem, particularly in the United States. This situation will probably only be solved when 'minors' can choose to live in places that are an acceptable alternative to a family situation with which they find themselves incompatible.

The style of living of working class groups, often with larger families in more cramped housing conditions, has led to a closer knowledge of the lives of the adults by their children. The observance of sexual relations is not as uncommon, nor as traumatic in its effects as some people have believed. The jobs of their parents are far more accessible in this group, and the child accompanying his father to work occurs more frequently.

Of course the notion of class group membership does not entail any uniformity of behaviour. Generalizations about class groups conceal wide differences. There is a large area of overlap in the interests and attitudes of people from various socio-economic groups and this has become increasingly true with the growing affluence of certain sections of the skilled and unskilled workers.

The changing agencies of socialization

The suggestion so far has been that the family and the school enabled the developing ideas of childhood to be given a reality. They separated children from adult society and in so doing gained an unparalleled power over the lives of the children. Aries' suggestion that the family has never previously occupied such a prominent place in society has been challenged from three directions. The sociological view of MacIver (1957) maintained that the functions of the preindustrial family have gradually been eroded. The economic, educational, health, religious, and recreational provisions of the home have been superseded by other institutions which have undermined the family's importance. The second line of attack has come from investigators who have bemoaned the breakup of the stable extended family of relatives who resided together for generation after generation. The third view is exemplified by the title of David Cooper's book *The Death of the Family* which sees families as undergoing a process of disintegration because of their failure to meet the psychological needs of their members.

It would seem that we have already had a glimpse of the preindustrial family as a situation of hard work for all its members, characterized by a high infant death rate that had little opportunity of meeting any but the most basic needs of children and adults. In a situation where there have never before been so few people living outside of a marriage relationship, it seems difficult to speak of the disintegration of the family, however desirable some people may feel this to be. Even the breakup of the extended family has been much slower and less widespread than many people imagined. The congruence in attitudes between parents and their adolescent children would suggest that schools may well have aided parents in keeping control of their children. We have noted before what a powerful socializing agent money can be, and the economic dependence of children on adults that has existed for the last 150 years has certainly contributed to an increase in family influence.

Family changes and the development of schooling have radically altered the development of individuals, and it is worth looking briefly at how the situation has changed. Of course school is not the only new extra-familial influence; the rise of the mass media, particularly television, and the perhaps accelerating social changes have made their own contributions to the changing child and adult. We have seen too how industrialization revolutionized the way of life of the population as people began to be controlled by work away from their homes.

Changes in family life

There is little doubt that there has been a gradual change in family life in which the nuclear family of parents and children spend an increasing amount of time together. As we noted some investigators had overestimated the extent to which the extended network of relatives and friends have disappeared. In 1924 Eileen Power wrote of English society in the Middle Ages:

The hurrying, scattering generation of today can hardly imagine the unmovable stability of the village of past centuries, when generation after generation grew from cradle to grave in the same houses, on the same cobbled streets, and folks of the same names were still friends as their fathers and grandfathers had been before them.

In their study of the Bethnal Green community in East London, Young and Willmott (1957) found that the extended family was still very important in the lives of the people. There was still a fairly common pattern in which the wife relied for support and friendship from her family and the husband continued to maintain close friendship with his mates. However, even in the working class community fathers were increasingly willing to share in looking after the children. The rehousing schemes and the movement out to the suburbs have applied further pressure in recent years to the break up of the kinship networks. Yet the increased mobility provided by the motor car and the use of the telephone have helped to reduce the effects of geographical isolation.

Until the nineteenth century, where men, women and children might be working sixteen hours a day away from the house, family life can hardly be said to have occurred at all for most people. Although parents had greater legal powers over their children in the past and fathers could beat their wives with even greater impunity than they do today, parental influence on children has actually increased in recent years (Musgrove, 1966). The situation in the cities at the end of the last century where bands of children were wandering the streets, stealing and fighting was one in which the 'family had lost control'.

The changing patterns of family life have been greeted with joy or despair, depending on the point of view of the writer, even though there is now a fair measure of agreement that the family has never before exerted such a strong influence on the development of individuals. Fletcher wrote his book (1962) as a champion of family life. In this book he maintains that marriages are at last becoming friendship relationships in which partners freely choose each other. Aries (1962) felt that the development of family life had 'imposed itself tyranically on people's consciousness'. It had cut off the individual from society. He looked back with regret at the way an open society, in which there was a free relationship between a large number of individuals, had been transformed into one containing a set of restricted private relationships between a few people in their individual housing units.

The growth of schooling

The separation of children from adults was achieved initially in the upper and middle classes by sending the children away to school. Early attempts to keep children away from the corrupting influence of servants failed by all accounts, because of the tremendous freedom at the boarding schools. Gradually the vague attempts at moral education were combined with harsh discipline, and the boarding schools were swelled by new recruits from middle class families.

It is true that industry demanded higher levels of technical proficiency from its workers but it is doubtful whether schools were needed to provide this. The old apprenticeship system was a far more efficient method of training. One factor in producing universal schooling may have been the increasing power of the working class which eventually brought the vote for all men in the latter part of the last century. However, we have seen that the large group of unemployed children was also a considerable prompt for more schools.

In 1802 the factory owners were made responsible for the provision of reading, writing and arithmetic lessons for the youngsters that they employed from 6am to 9pm But in 1841 33 per cent of men and 49 per cent of women still just made a mark when signing the marriage register. The factory schools were a farce; often the teachers were unable to write themselves (Musgrave, 1968). It was not until 1840 that the first attempts were made to provide teacher training.

By 1865, of the child population between the ages of 3 and 12, 6 per cent were at work and 40 per cent attended school. The majority then were left to roam the streets.

Elementary education was only made universally available in England in 1870 although it was not enforced legally. Even in 1922 there were 70,000 children on half-time attendance in the agricultural areas. In areas where the labour market needed workers, schools took second place.

Childhood education helped to transform the lives of children by separating them from the adult world. It also made vast inroads into the literacy problem. By 1891 the number making their mark on the marriage register had decreased to 6 per cent of men and 7 per cent of women.

This is the recent educational past of this country. It is only a hundred years since universal primary education was made available to the working class. The middle and upper classes monopolized the fee-paying secondary schools and the schools helped to cement the class differences in society. It was not until after the first world war that secondary education was made compulsory for all children, but by that time class differences in attitudes towards education had become firmly entrenched. Whatever the implications of the Bullock Report (1975) for the problems of illiteracy, there is little doubt that education over the last hundred years has created entirely new opportunities in the development of the people of this country.

Social change

I have looked at some of the changes that have occurred in the institutions of society. Work, family and school together embody a pattern of life that is immeasurably different from that which surrounded individuals even a hundred years ago. I mentioned how Darwin's theory of evolution was applied not only to the new science of psychology but also by social theorists. As applied to the development of social institutions it provided them with an irresistible opportunity to believe that 'evolution' of their culture represented the highest point of civilized life. We can imagine the dinosaur surveying his huge beautiful frame and attempting a rapid shuffle of his feet before exclaiming 'Who's Ali? Look at me! I'm the greatest.' Unfortunately, environmental conditions changed more quickly than he could. In the same way, social, political, economic and educational institutions which adapted to the historic conditions of the past may persist for a while after the conditions which created them have been radically altered.

It has been argued, for example, that the nuclear family of parents and children is ideally suited to a consumer society. It involves the consumption of the maximum number of goods (Phillips, 1969). If the economic situation of the country alters, new patterns of living may be forced upon us that are more suited to a reduction in consumption. Whatever our future, it is clear that each change in the institutions of our society will provoke a corresponding reaction in the lives of its citizens.

5
Different groups, different peoples

In the last chapter, I looked at the changes in the ways individuals have experienced their development in recent history. I drew mainly on the social changes that have occurred in this country, but also incorporated the emergence of notions about life stages that have arisen in other countries. Industrialization produced a pattern of urban living and a demand for schooling that have created similarities in the development of the individuals of industrialized nations. However, the idiosyncracies in the forces for social change in each country have produced differences in the types of institutions and in the lives of the people living there (see C5).

Kandel and Lesser (1972) in their book *Youth in Two Worlds* compared groups of young people drawn from rural, urban and regional schools in the United States and Denmark. In agreement with several other recent studies, they found no evidence in either country for a gap in values between generations. Neither was there a conflict between home and peer group. The children who felt most settled at home actually had the greatest peer group involvement. They did notice that there was a greater tendency in the Danish families for the adults and children to make decisions together. The Danish children seemed more independent at an earlier age and tended to turn to their friends more frequently for advice;

they treated them as other adults. Although the American children had access to more money, these authors felt that parents in the United States treated their 'adolescents' as 'children' for a considerably longer period than in Denmark. One of the institutional differences between the countries is reflected in the shorter average period of schooling that the children receive in Denmark, and we can speculate on the role of the school in prolonging childhood in the USA. However, in comparing only two groups, it is impossible to give an explanation of the differences that are found with any certainty. The difference might equally be due to the differences in authority structure within the family.

We have seen how an attempt to trace the changes in human development led us to discuss the different effects of social change on groups within the country. I used the terms 'nobility', 'middle class', 'working class' to denote categories of people whose lives were shaped in diverse ways. In a more detailed account of the way individuals were altered by the processes of history, we would need to look far more carefully at regional variations and at the difference between urban and rural patterns of living. We would find that broad categories were inadequate to describe the range of variations between people. However, studies that look for 'class differences' in attitudes or childrearing practices often use the two categories 'middle class' and 'working class' and obscure the diversity of behaviour that occurs within one group of people characterized by their occupations.

In this chapter I want to look at some of the differences in the lives of individuals who grow up in different parts of the world and who form different groups of a particular society. Levine (1970) has argued that crosscultural and subcultural studies should be treated together in psychology. They both ask and answer questions about the way different influences affect the development of individuals. However, in considering these issues together, we have to bear in mind that the behaviour of the particular group can only be interpreted in relation to the society in which it exists. In some Greek villages the children are mercilessly teased and taunted by their parents as part of a total childrearing pattern (Friedl, 1962), yet this behaviour produced no discernible adverse effects on the childrens' development. It is quite possible that if groups of children were treated in this way in England, they might grow up to show signs of disturbance. Each individual is not only affected by his own socializing experiences, but also by the attitudes of those around him. The relationship between the parts of a social system is indicated too by the way changes in one practice or institution of a society may reverberate throughout the social fabric. 'Culture contact' with Western nations sometimes had far-reaching consequences for other societies.

It is sometimes assumed that life in preliterate societies is relatively uniform, yet within the so-called 'primitive' societies described by anthropologists, different individuals often fulfilled different functions within the group and experienced their own quality of life. This has applied particularly to the differences in the lives of men and women and we will consider later some of the issues raised by the differences in sex role behaviour that occur in societies.

In taking a leap into social history, I was aware of the problems that are associated with establishing historical facts. Each book that I read represented the 'facts' of industrialization in different ways and I had to attempt to assess the probability that reported changes had actually occurred. If, as I maintain, people are constantly changing, then the psychologist of human development has no choice but to come to terms with the problems associated with establishing the effect of social change. In a similar way, the type of knowledge that can be derived from studies of remote peoples may seem less well substantiated than the more carefully documented results of laboratory experiment or a survey using a standard interview. However, if we feel that it is important to understand the way these people spend their lives, then we have to accept the difficulties involved in documenting them. It is appropriate to consider, next, some of the problems that are involved in examining the way of life of different cultural groups and why such investigations might be important in increasing our understanding of human development.

Research in other cultures: problems and purposes

In reviewing the contribution of crosscultural studies to psychological knowledge, Levine (1970) concluded: 'Altogether, the impression is one of wasted effort.' Similarly, Danziger (1971) commented on the crosscultural endeavour: 'Two decades of effort have yielded little but an improved awareness of the many pitfalls that await the research worker in this area.' In attempting to derive psychological studies from the fascinating subject matter of anthropology, psychologists seem to have lost their way. Throughout this book, I have stressed the need for psychology to take account of related disciplines, and nowhere is this more relevant than in the attempts to compare individual development in different cultural settings. In order to understand the growth of the individual in one's own society, one needs to have an understanding of the way the society is structured. In comparing aspects of different societies, one needs to comprehend the significance of each element of behaviour in terms of the society in which it occurs. I mentioned earlier how teasing behaviour may be differently interpreted in Greece and England. Lévi-Strauss (1967) is an anthropologist who has emphasized the importance of looking at the structure of societies. He maintains that the 'social facts we study are manifested by societies each of which is a total entity, concrete and cohesive.' (See B5)

Problems of assessment
In Chapter 3, we noted the difficulty of establishing persisting personality traits in individuals (see too D3). Yet psychologists have attempted to relate the development of traits such as aggression and dependency to the childrearing practices of different societies (Whiting and Child, 1953). Even where differences between cultures have emerged, these become

doubly difficult to interpret when the variables involved represent traits that have been shown to have little meaning as they are conventionally measured.

The issues which relate to the problems of personality assessment apply to many of the psychological studies of different cultural groups. Unfortunately, anthropologists have in recent years begun to employ some dubious psychological techniques in their own investigations. Projective tests, such as the Rorschach inkblots, present a picture or design to an individual, who then is expected to tell a story or say what the design represents. The ambiguity of the situation is meant to enable different individuals to interpret what they see in ways that are characteristic of their personalities. This technique derives from the psychoanalytic view that everything you do or say, including slips of the pen, is to be interpreted as a possible sign of inner personality conflict. Whilst it is relatively easy to work out a coherent description of the personality of an individual from the way he sees inkblots or the stories he tells in response to different pictures, it is very difficult to establish whether these descriptions are really valid. It is extremely dubious to attempt to establish the preoccupations of an individual from a remote tribe from the stories he tells in response to a set of pictures that have been thought to be meaningful by someone from a totally different culture.

The Truk are a cultural group from Micronesia who were described by Gladwin and Sarason (1953) in their book *Truk: Man in Paradise*. They enjoyed an absence of sexual restraint before marriage and this was taken to indicate that the Trukese had little anxiety about sex. However, the results of projective tests were said to show that the people really had considerable sexual conflict. Unfortunately, the people seem to have been placed in a 'Catch 22' situation where freedom of sexual behaviour was taken as indicating lack of anxiety, yet concern with sexual themes in the interpretation of test material was assumed to indicate high anxiety level. One man's enjoyment of freedom is another man's preoccupation with restraint. The relevance of studies such as these is that they indicate the difficulty encountered in trying to disprove a particular psychological view. In this case the proponents of adolescence as a universal period of 'storm and stress' might feel that they would find it if they probed deeply enough.

The introduction of assessment techniques followed criticism of the subjective nature of the descriptions of early anthropologists. When they described the child-rearing practices, the personality characteristics or behaviour of individuals of a society, it was often felt that they were making broad generalizations based on incautious sampling. The Ganda of East Africa had been described as abruptly weaning their children and then sending them to be reared by their grandmothers. Ainsworth (1967) set off in the hope of comparing these infants before and after separation with the intention of discovering how children reacted to a culturally accepted breach of their attachments. After she had arrived, she discovered to her disappointment that such separation was a very infrequent practice.

Adequate sampling of the society under investigation represents a particularly difficult problem. Where subcultural groups are present, the lives of each group need to be treated separately if development within the culture is to be adequately analysed.

In this book, I have scrupulously avoided the notion that there is an average person whose behaviour is worth considering. The concept of personality should refer to an individual whose personal circumstances, relationships and organizations can be understood. The notion of 'national character' or 'modal personality' seems to be of dubious value to psychology, though it may make amusing subject matter for after dinner jokes.

Ervin (1964) gave a personality test to sixty-four bilingual Frenchmen, once in English and once in French. He noted that their personalities shifted in accordance with national stereotypes, depending on which language they used. Personality is understandable in the context of a particular group in a particular society in a particular language. The idea of comparing the personalities of people in different cultures may be doomed to failure. The behaviour of an individual, like the words he uses, are signs that are completely understandable only in the context in which they are learned and used. The anthropologist, as Lévi-Strauss suggests, may study the way these signs are related to each other and to the institutions of a society to form a total system. The psychologist may study, for example, the way these signs are learned and what their significance is in their context and the consequences within a particular culture for deviating from cultural roles and norms.

Anthropology as a human activity
A recurrent problem in psychological research involves the way the experimenter influences the results of his studies. In experiments in social psychology the subjects may be influenced by the way the psychologist looks, how he talks, whether he is a man or woman. The subject of an experiment may be thinking: 'What does he want me to do?' or 'How can I make the experiment give him the "right" answer?' The individual who sets off from one society with a particular set of values and attitudes is in a difficult situation when he comes to attempt an objective assessment of the people he has come to study. In his study of the people of the Trobriand islands, Malinowski attempted to show that the oedipal conflict of rivalry with father for the love of the mother was not a universal stage through which all young boys passed and he sets out his findings in an impressively dispassionate style. Malinowski's diaries were published posthumously in 1967 and while his scientific writings must be assessed on their own merit certain passages in the diaries suggest that the objectivity of his descriptions may have become strained at times. They even supply his opponents with the last laugh for they might suggest that he was writing about his own oedipal feelings when he said: 'At last I begin to feel a deep strong longing for mother in my innermost being ... mother is the only person I care for really and am truly worried about.' He had this to say of the subjects of his study: 'I see the life of the natives as utterly devoid of interest or importance, something as remote from me as the life of a dog.' He found himself

'strongly hating the niggers.' Evidently he felt at that time, in his cultural isolation, that there was little point to the study of anthropology.

Malinowski was subsequently hailed as one of the first field-workers to introduce the ideas of participant observation into anthropology (Wax, 1972). The idea he propounded, though hardly practised, was that the investigator should become as closely involved as possible in the life of the community. In fact, he preferred to be treated as a village elder with a number of servants. His diaries are at some points a parody of civilized man surveying the savage. While he was taking some pictures of a group of girls he relates: 'I made one or two coarse jokes and one bloody nigger made a disapproving remark, whereupon I cursed them and was highly irritated. I managed to control myself on the spot, but I was terribly vexed by the fact that the nigger had dared to speak to me in this manner.'

Margaret Mead (1973) took a very different view of her investigations into remote cultures. She dedicated her recent autobiography to 'the eight peoples who have admitted me to their lives'. She had, too, a clear purpose in her investigations: 'I have spent most of my life studying the lives of other peoples, faraway peoples, so that Americans might better understand themselves.' In the course of her life, though, there were periods of particular strain which may have affected her attitude to her research. She had always been very keen to have a child, but was told by a specialist that she was unable to have children. She was immediately sent to study a tribe of ex-cannibals, the Mundugumor, whose lives she found distasteful: 'The Mundugumor presented a harsh contrast to the Arapesh, whose whole meager and hardworking lives were devoted to growing their children. In Mundugumor homes sleeping babies were hung in rough textured baskets in a dark place against the wall, and when a baby cried, someone would scratch gratingly on the outside of the basket ... I simply felt repelled.' In her reports she chose to describe the Arapesh after the colonial period, yet referred to the Mundugumor as if they still practised their old forms of warfare.

She thus exaggerated the differences between them. Before the advent of colonization, the Arapesh had in fact been quite warlike. Half of the older men claimed to have killed at least one person (Fortune, 1939). Mead's main thesis at that time was that men and women could adopt very similar sex roles or even reverse the current American stereotypes. This argument for diversity of sex-role behaviour was not really affected by the particular slice of time from which she chose to sample her data. She did in fact later become a mother and a grandmother, and one can speculate – if one wishes – on how this might have related to the change in her attitude to sex differences between the publication of her two books, *Sex and Temperament in Three Societies* (1935) and *Male and Female* (1949). In the later book she adopted the view that women do have one role in life that is more 'natural' than others.

Studying cultures in the process of change

All cultures change, some more slowly than others. This is an inevitable result of their changing population and the changing nature of their environment. When an anthropologist samples the life of a society, even over a period of a year or more, it is extremely difficult to assess the extent to which historical forces have contributed to the present nature of that society. This may lead to considerable misinterpretation of the lives of the people under scrutiny. The Aymara Indians of Bolivia and Peru were described as a submissive, gloomy, anxious people who were extremely mistrustful and spent much of their time in muting their cares with alcohol and cocaine. However, such a description may be less a reflection of the way their society trained them than of the effect on them of the decimation of their number by 8,000,000 during the Spanish occupation, their subordination to the ruling class of Mestizos and the fact that the hated Mestizos were often used by the observers as interpreters. Later studies noted that where the traditional social units survived in the villages, these people were far more optimistic and were politically active (Barnouw, 1973).

By the time anthropologists got round to studying 'other peoples', their cultures had often been brutally affected by the colonial powers. As a Central American Indian explained to Ruth Benedict (1935): 'In the beginning God gave to every people a cup, a cup of clay, and from this cup they drank their life. They all dipped in the water but their cups were different. Our cup is broken now. It has passed away.' In some cases, the effects of breaking the culture of a people was so drastic, that they resolved to go out of production. Of the Marquesan culture Linton (1939) wrote:

Theirs was a perfectly deliberate measure; the people preferred extinction to subjection. I visited many villages populated entirely by persons of middle age to old age without a single child in the group. On Tahuata, the island next to the one on which I was living, there were over two hundred deaths for every birth.

The Samoans were said to be little affected by the advent of the missionaries and colonists (Mead, 1928). However, ritual tattooing and warfare had been abolished. The class of master craftsmen had disappeared through the advent of Western technology, as had the life and death powers that household heads had over their families. School had been introduced for children between the ages of six and twelve. On occasion sexual lapses by daughters had been punished by severe beatings and shaving of the offender's head. Seen in this light the sexual freedom of the young may have been partially produced by the diminution of family authority.

I suggested that changes in one aspect of a social structure might affect the whole social system. In some cultures men were separated from women after puberty to form a war group. This separation was associated with a complex initiation into the rituals and folklore of the society. After a period in this 'age-grade', the young men returned back to the mainstream of their society to marry and work the land. The banning of warfare between neighbouring groups rendered much of the social organization of such societies pointless and where they survived their whole society was radically disrupted.

Lévi-Strauss sees one of the main purposes of his subject as creating the 'anthropological doubt'. It causes us to question the structure and functioning of our own society; to see it as offering one of many solutions to the problems of organizing a cooperative life, of raising children and of facing death. Unfortunately, much of the subject matter of anthropology was destroyed before the 'anthropological doubt' became widespread. The genocide of many of the indigenous peoples of South and North America is evidence of the failure of 'doubt' to restrain the 'certainty' that people have had about the unique importance of their own way of life.

The fact that societies are in a constant process of change makes it extremely difficult to interpret any correlation between child-training practices and later adult behaviour. If we accept that a culture is an independent network that evolves over time, then cross-cultural surveys can only suggest possibilities about the way early experience determines later development. 'To test generalizations about change, it is necessary to study societies during the process of change' (Levine, 1970).

Explanations of cross-cultural differences
D'Andrade (1966) summarized in a neat way the types of argument that are put forward to explain the occurrence of particular practices in a society. *Historical* explanations seek to explain a practice as arising in response to forces occurring at a particular time in history which are perpetuated by the culture, even though conditions may have changed. *Structuralist* interpretations describe the way the aspects of a society under consideration are interrelated with other practices and institutions. A *functionalist* view looks for the ways in which the cultural life of a community is enhanced by the occurrence of the practice. Finally, what D'Andrade terms a *reductionist* view seeks to explain a mode of behaviour in a culture in terms of its psychological significance for the individual, rather than in terms of the relationship of the indi-

vidual with his society. As we shall see, several of these explanations may operate together to help us to gain a total picture of the significance of a particular mode of behaviour.

Differences in the life cycle

Ruth Benedict (1938) presented a scheme for interpreting the different courses of development in different societies. They could be differentiated by the degree to which they stressed development of the individual as a gradual, continuous process, or as separated into a series of discrete stages. She thought that American society, of that time, involved a discontinuous development that demanded a rapid switch in behaviour at the termination of adolescence in three ways. The American adolescent was expected to change from a nonresponsible status role, in which he made no contribution to the economy of the family, to a responsible position as a provider for his own family. He had to cease his submission to adults and become dominant over his own children, and he had to enter the world of adult sexuality from the world of childhood chastity.

The pattern of growth of American youth was contrasted with the life-style of the Cheyenne Indians, who presented the male child with a bow and arrow at birth. As soon as his aim was adequate, the boy contributed to the family meals. His offerings were accepted as equal in importance to those of his father. As his skill and strength improved, he progressed along a graded food chain until he brought home his first buffalo. At that point, he had become a man. The way of life of the Cheyenne Indians was paralleled by the continuities in many cultures, where in addition to economic responsibility, children conventionally had an easy relationship of equality with at least some adults and a gradual development of sexuality.

Benedict was probably observing the challenges faced by only a minority of American adolescents. She would have noted other styles of living if she had looked beyond the restrictions of her own subcultural group. However, we have

111

seen how she was noticing the discontinuities that have emerged in the industrialized nations, which have progressively exaggerated the stage of childhood in the development of their institutions.

Commenting on the data from the various cultures of the world, Goodman (1967) noted that 'People rarely dichotomize between children and adults as we do and even fewer conceive of a murky transitional phase of adolescence ... The western concept of the child as a creature of emotions, physically fragile and easily damaged is almost without parallel.' However, the spread of Western industrial culture and institutions has, of course, meant that many more people share in the 'Western' pattern of development than did even seventy years ago. In some communities which do conceive of a world of childhood, the child may be thought to take part in two worlds. The Igbo of Nigeria expect children to take an active part in all the social and economic activities of their parents, although the society recognizes that children also have a separate life which differentiates them from adults.

In her own studies of urban children in Japan and the United States, Goodman found that children aged five had a remarkable grasp of the society's basic culture and structure. She felt that they demonstrated that they were capable of fitting into the adult society, although they would be excluded from full participation for many years.

Perhaps the groups who come closest to perceiving development as a continuous process are those that have developed the idea that the souls of ancestors return as new born infants of the same family. The Balinese conceived of this cycle as being repeated every fourth generation. In their terms, great grandparents and great grandchildren were the same generation and both are nearer the spirit world than the middle-aged. It was felt to be rather presumptuous for great grandparents to linger on when they could literally make way for the next generation. All age groups in the society participated together in all activities: 'The distinction between the most gifted and least gifted is muted by the fact that everyone participates, the distinction between the child and adult – as performer, as

112

actor, as musician – is lost except in those cases where the distinction is ritual.' (Mead and Wolfenstein, 1955)

A case of discontinuity

Benedict had been prompted to write her article in response to information about the Manus culture in which children exhibit an extremely discontinuous development. When they were first studied in 1930, they were a lagoon society building their dwellings on stilts. The children had to be trained with great solicitude for their lives above the deep water. Once they had mastered the necessary physical skills, childhood was regarded as a period of extended play, in which they were given complete emotional freedom. The demands of mothers could be disregarded with equanimity though they did respond to the fathers, who were described as dominant but tender, solicitous and indulgent guardians. After the first year, in which the mother and child were shut up together in the house, the father took charge of the offspring and the mother became little more than a household slave.

Separation of boys from girls might occur from the age of eight and soon afterwards marriage partners were selected. From then until marriage, the marriage partner or members of his or her family had to be scrupulously avoided. There was some sex play before the rigid separation of the sexes, but subsequently chastity of women was rigidly enforced. The period between betrothal and marriage, particularly for the girl, was one of preparation for her economic role. The adolescent boys had previously been involved in war and the capture of women from neighbouring groups to use as prostitutes, but by 1930 this had been outlawed and they usually went away for a period to work on ships or in service on the mainland. When the boys returned, their lives became one of economic bondage. They had to work to pay their uncles back for the bride price. The familial tie was much stronger to his sister than to his bride. Living adjacent to his sister, his new wife came into a situation of constant friction, just as 'she and her sisters had hated her brother's wife' (Mead, 1930). After an elaborate marriage ceremony, the

113

woman is left with her husband to experience sex she has been conditioned to fear and embark on a marriage relationship, bereft of tenderness and affection, in which even her offspring will be 'hers' for only a year. The family unit was maintained by the strict economic obligations that they had to their kin and the rigid supervision that they believed was exercised over their economic and sexual lives by their recently dead ancestors.

Age-sets

A few societies, mainly in Africa, separate boys into various groups according to age, and these groups represent abrupt discontinuities in the status position of males. The first age-set among the Nandi of Kenya is comprised of all boys under twelve years old. After an initiation ritual, boys advance to the second age-set, are called 'junior warriors', and retain this status for a further four years. They then progress to a 'senior warrior' status and after their four years national service, they are permitted to marry and enter into the daily life and work in their villages, free of the demands of warfare (Hollis, 1909). Not all age-sets serve functions that are related to warfare. The Nyakajusa of Tanzania divide up the boys according to the economic activity in which they are expected to engage. From six to twelve years, these boys tend the herds of their fathers' cattle. At twelve, they join a boys' village, from which they are expected to cultivate the gardens of their parents and learn the basis of cooperative living. At the age of twenty to twenty-five, they inherit a plot of land, marry and bring their wives to the village. When a further period has elapsed, these young men are given full political autonomy in their village and the process starts again with their own offspring. The cooperative nature of the social organization of the village transcends the ties of kinship for these people, either with their parents or with their own children. The formation of age-sets, whilst imposing discontinuities on the development and status of the individuals, can be seen as a formal plan for solving the economic or security preoccupations of a particular group (Wilson, 1951).

114

The process of puberty

The onset of puberty is more marked for girls than boys because of menstruation. In some groups, such as the Carrier Indians of British Columbia, menarche was associated with a three year period of isolation, during which the girl was regarded as a source of evil. However, the Apache regarded such girls as provided with supernatural powers of healing.

Many cultures permit a gradual change from infantile sexual interests to the more urgent sexual exploits of the pubertal years. In the Samoan culture, where girls are responsible for taking care of the next younger sibling, adolescence passes as a period of increased experimentation. The Trobriand islanders were another group characterized by a permissive attitude to infantile sex play which gradually transformed into adult sexuality. A group of boys shared a 'bachelor house', where they lived with their girlfriends before adopting a more stable form of marriage.

Developmental continuity does not necessitate the individual in unlearning any of his previous behaviour patterns. But in their elaborate rules for marriage, most societies, even those that practise prior sexual license, have expected their partners to tend towards fidelity.

Initiation rituals

Among the societies which practise age-setting are some which mark the adoption of adult status in a drastic way, by means of initiation rites. Although this status change may be associated with the onset of the process of puberty, particularly for girls, in others it may not coincide with this process at all. An extreme example of initiation rites occurred among the Arunta of Central Australia. Boys were taken initially from their home camp by older men at about the age of twelve, and over a period of several years they were given detailed religious instruction and put through a set of four painful ordeals. The boys were said to look forward to the start of this process, but that may be because they didn't know what they were in for. To boost the initiate's strength the men first smeared him with their own blood and then they pierced the nasal septum and knocked out one of his front teeth. After a year's seclusion the boys were brought back and circumcised whilst lying on a human table formed by young adults. When he was fully healed, he was welcomed back from seclusion by his family and received as an adult. However the process was not over yet. During the next two years, the novice was given further instruction and this was followed by a sub-incision ceremony in which the uretha was slit open along the length of the penis. Twelve months later, however, the last stage was finally performed, in which ceremonial cuts could be made in the novice's back and possibly on his arms, thighs and lower abdomen. After he had received his stripes, the Arunta man was free to marry. Each part of the initiation was explained by the Arunta in terms of its religious, magical and symbolic significance (Williams, 1972).

When one has finished gaping in amazement at these practices, one is left wondering how such a complex and apparently painful process ever got started and how it persisted once it has begun. The power of individual cultures to transmit idiosyncratic practices which bear no direct relationship to biological necessity is astonishing.

Arunta girls escaped comparatively lightly. During a week of seclusion at the first sign of puberty, they were given details of sex and marriage behaviour. After a ritual bath, an Arunta girl was declared a woman. If her marriage had been pre-arranged, she was immediately handed over to her husband's family. The adult men confirmed her womanly status by making love to her. If a marriage had not been arranged, then the young woman could be involved in further ceremonies during which her vulva and hymen were cut and her nose pierced.

Various explanations have been proposed for the initiation rituals observed by some groups. Cohen (1964) has related the presence of such rituals to the concern of a society with training individuals to develop close emotional ties with others. The college fraternities of America often incorporate some form of discomforting or degrading initiation. A secret rite, which might appear silly to outsiders, often marks the acceptance of members into Masonic lodges. However, the fact that initiation rites are associated with an increased attachment to the group does not explain why ritual should increase group interdependence. To do that, we need to look at a psychological view such as Festinger's (1962) theory of cognitive dissonance (see B1 and B3). The painful experience may produce a conflict (or 'dissonance') between attachment to and rejection of the group which is resolved by minimizing the pain and increasing the value of the group.

Other suggested explanations of male mutilation of their sex organs invoke the notion of womb envy. It is said that men attempt to reproduce the signs of menstruation in response to their jealousy of women's procreative abilities. One may need to give an explanation of why it is specifically the sex organs that are cut, but this may equally occur because of the presumed relationship between puberty and adult status.

Whiting (1964) developed a complex argument to explain the presence of male initiation rites. He noticed that societies in which they occurred often involved people in tropical areas which have little protein food. This led to prolonged breast-feeding and an arrangement where husbands had several wives. They tended to live with the non-lactating ones. The close infant-mother relationship that ensued promoted an identification of boys with their mothers, which could only be broken by a drastic initiation ceremony into a male cult. Partial support for this type of suggestion is given by the ceremonial dragging away of the Arunta boy from the reluctant women folk that marks the start of their initiation. However, as we shall see, evidence from one-parent families in our culture does not support the notion that a female identification necessarily occurs in such boys.

Men and women

Whilst most societies fail to recognize strict distinctions between children and adults, most practise some role division between the sexes.

In an attempt to provide a simple account of the differences

117

between the behaviour of men and women, investigators have stressed one of two explanations. Like Hutt (1972) they set out to state 'the case for the biological bases of psychological sex differences'. Alternatively, following Mead (1935) they maintain that 'we may say that many if not all the personality traits we have called masculine and feminine are as lightly linked to sex as are the clothing, manners and headdress that a society at a given period assigns to either sex.'

Each view places a different emphasis on the role of parents in teaching their children to exhibit masculine or feminine behaviour. A view that sex differences in behaviour are closely linked to biological differences in the brain or hormonal composition of the body tends to imply that parents are passive observers of the process of sex differentiation. Thus Nash (1970) suggested that 'although sex differences are known to exist extensively, the fact has had surprisingly little influence on practice in childrearing or in education. Boys and girls are in general treated as if no difference existed between them.' The notion that stresses the importance of training boys to be boyish and girls to be girlish places the responsibility for teaching on parents and others through the processes of instrumental conditioning or modelling (see B1 and D3).

Adherents to either position are also naturally drawn to adopt one or other stance on the issue of Women's Liberation. Simone de Beauvoir, as a founding mother of the modern revival of the women's movement, described women in these terms: 'It is civilization as a whole that produces this creature intermediate between male and eunuch, which is described as feminine.' However, Nash had this to say on the clamour for equal occupational opportunity: 'If a woman cannot bring some unique contribution to engineering then she is misplaced in this profession ... of course the feminist may insist that she has a unique contribution to make to any profession, including engineering; then let her define it.' Clearly all that is asked by the proponents of basic human rights for women is that their contributions should be assessed on the same terms as those of men.

The argument for the biological basis for sex differences has been used in a further way. It has been said that women are 'naturally' disposed to be passive, submissive and nurturing while men have to be aggressive and dominant. Anthony Storr (1968), who sees the biological nature of men and women as exemplified by the active sperm rushing aggressively towards the passively receptive ovum, regards dominant women who are more interested in a career than in child care as psychologically sick. In this context one of the virtues of the cross-cultural method is that it may demonstrate that what is regarded as deviant or 'sick' in one society may in another be regarded as common practice.

There are a few problems of definition that we need to consider when talking about male and female behaviour. We talk of sex identity to refer to the gender or sex a person thinks of himself as. There seem to be relatively few individuals who conceive of themselves as a different gender to their biological sex, unless they have been born with misleading external genitals. A male homosexual thinks of himself as a man and a lesbian thinks of herself as a woman. We speak of sex-role behaviour to describe the pattern of behaviour that is conventionally expected of an individual of a particular sex. This notion raises considerable problems because different groups within the same society have different ideas of what is masculine or feminine behaviour. There is little point in describing an individual from one group according to the standards of masculinity or femininity of a different group. Lastly, we need to invoke the notion of sexual-orientation to describe the inclination of a person who chooses sexual partners predominantly from the same sex or from both sexes or from the opposite sex.

We will turn now to evidence concerning the relative contribution of sex hormones, sex genes and upbringing on the eventual temperament of men and women. I will confine myself to the areas of personal and social behaviour. Attempts to define cognitive differences between the sexes are treated elsewhere (see Hutt, 1972). However, as I have suggested before, slight differences that are found between large groups of men and women on certain intellectual tasks are relatively meaningless when applied to a profile of capabilities of one man or woman.

Mistaken identity

Occasionally children are born whose external genitals do not correspond with their internal sexual composition and hence hormonally and genetically may be of the opposite sex. Follow up studies of these children suggest that they behave in all respects according to the sex to which they were initially assigned (Hampson, 1965). Hampson and his associates noted that a child could be reassigned to a different sex before the age of three fairly successfully, but once a child had developed a sexual identity, reassignment of sex produced extreme psychological disturbance. The only successful solution was to alter the internal anatomic sex by means of surgery and hormonal replacement therapy to conform to the sex in which they were reared. Such studies were taken as confirming that masculine or feminine identity was solely determined by the way children are brought up.

However, there have been other groups of children whose development has thrown some doubt on the strength of this argument. In the United States an artificial hormone preparation, 'progestin', was prescribed to women in an effort to stave off repeated miscarriages. Inside the womb these children were unwittingly subjected to doses of male hormone which produced a considerable number of little girls who had enlarged clitori or partially fused labia. Money and Erhardt (1968) followed up nine of the girls whose genitalia had been masculinized and another one whose mother received the treatment, but who had been born anatomically normal. Although all the children thought of themselves as female, nine out of the ten children were considered to be tomboys, either by themselves or their mothers. Similar results were obtained on a group of women who had developed a defect of the adrenal gland which caused the secretion of male hormones before and after birth. When untreated such a disorder speeds up the rate of sexual development and may bring puberty forward to the age of five or six. The development of

120

cortisone therapy in the 1950s enabled the adrenal glands to be partially switched off. Brecher (1970) commented: 'Girls that had been masculinized before birth by male hormones from their own adrenal glands were much more tomboyish than girls of the same age, intelligence and socio-economic class in a control group.' Taken together these studies suggest limited support for hormonal involvement in the development of sex-role behaviour, though not on sexual identity. All these girls thought of themselves as girls. However, experimental results on a group likely to be treated from birth in an idiosyncratic way cannot confirm conclusively that hormones do play a part.

Other psychological results
Other studies indicate that boys and girls are treated in different ways and that the way they are treated affects their sex-role behaviour. Of immediate relevance is research by Sears *et al* (1965). They found that girls who adopted more masculine behaviour according to the scales administered by the experimenters tended to have a warm, interactive, permissive and understanding relationship with their fathers. An appreciation of their fathers presumably led them to share in some of his role behaviour. Such behaviour was also frequently affected by the sex of an older sibling. Where the older child was of the opposite sex, the younger child veered towards their sex-role behaviour (Rosenberg, 1968). These results fit in neatly with the ideas on modelling that we discussed in Chapter 2. We might expect the effect of family models to disappear as the child becomes older and is exposed to a wider range of models.

That boys and girls are treated in different ways in American and English society is not only a common observation but is actually confirmed by a number of studies. Girls tend to receive more affection, and are spoken to more frequently by their mothers. They are permitted to be more dependent, but the greatest difference seems to be in the parental intolerance towards any aggression they display (Sears *et al*, 1957).

The answers we get about male and female role behaviour from cross-cultural studies depend on the questions that we ask. In her analysis of the behaviour of three societies in 1935, Margaret Mead approached the problem by attempting to discover whether there was any society in which sex roles ran counter to current American practice.

The problem of assessing American norms of masculinity and femininity is very great. Clearly it is not sufficient to look at a Hollywood stereotype or at some average behaviour for the whole society. The range of variation amongst different groups in her society needed to be known before she could make any accurate comparison. However, she did find societies that seemed to function and persist whilst their men and women acted out roles that contrasted markedly with her view of the American stereotype. Despite objections to her studies which have already been mentioned, it does seem that the Arapesh exhibited a pattern in which men and women shared cooperatively in the rearing of the children and tended to be a relatively gentle people. The Mundugumor had little interest in children and both sexes were said to be violent and aggressively sexed. They took little interest in childbirth and the practice that seems to have created general family hostility involved fathers swapping their daughters to obtain an extra wife whilst sons need to swap a sister for a wife of their own. The Tchambali seemed to reverse sex roles. The women worked the land and controlled the family economy whilst the men sat in groups chatting and adorning themselves. The discovery of these groups all living within a radius of a hundred miles of each other led to the conclusion that sex-role divisions must be relatively easily modifiable by cultural change. In her later analysis in 1949, where she included data from four other cultures she was seeking a much more general solution. She was looking for general trends in societies which might lead her to a conclusion about what 'on the average' was the 'natural' role for women. This second book concluded that women were more nurturing than men, expressed their creativity in childrearing and childbirth, and were superior in intellectual activities which required intuition. Fatherhood was said to be a 'social invention' whilst motherhood was a biological inclination. A view which attempts to determine the 'natural' propensities of men and women by taking a poll of the average mode of behaviour of people implies that groups are 'going against nature' if they emphasize a sex-role division other than one in which dominant sexually energetic men live with passive receptive nurturant women.

Now it seems to me that the conclusions of the first question are inescapable and demand a different type of explanation from the results of the second study. If subgroups within one society or groups from another society are able to adopt different patterns of sex-role behaviour then this implies that the particular pattern of behaviour in our society is not fixed by individual biology. In fact sex roles have changed considerably in recent years. Newson and Newson (1974) reported that 52 per cent of their all-class sample of men felt they should take an equal share in chores associated with looking after babies when they were at home. The most participant were shop and clerical workers, then professional people, and last were unskilled workers. Even in this last group the numbers of 'non-participant' men was only 6 per cent by the time the children were four years old. This contrasts sharply with the view of traditional working-class relationships suggested by Klein (1965). In looking for any trend towards conformity in the sex-role behaviour in various countries of the world we need to seek an explanation which involves factors other than biological propensities.

Clearly there are situations where a division of labour results from the extra size and strength of men. It is also clear that women give birth to children and, in most societies of the world, need to breast feed them. It is quite possible that these simple facts gave rise to a pattern of development in many societies which, once enshrined by the culture, enabled men to form not only a physically but also a politically dominant group. Tiger (1970) seeks to explain the political dominance of men in many societies of the world by their greater propensity to form strong group bonds. There is however little evidence for this proposition. In a large sample of American men and women Booth (1972) found that women made a larger number of relationships than men and that these tended to be deeper and more lasting.

Family and kinship

Societies present such a tremendous variety of types of family organization that it becomes meaningless to compare families in different societies until we understand exactly what is meant by a family in a particular society. Most groups recognize two types of family relationship, a blood tie (or consanguineal relationship) and a marriage bond. People related by marriage are termed affines. The consanguineal and affinal relationships that a particular society regard as important represent the kinship pattern of that society. This pattern of kinship is associated with a set of duties and rights that regulate the interactions of individuals.

Kinship patterns aren't always as easy to work out as might seem at first sight. The Trobriand islanders, at the time they were studied by Malinowski, did not recognize the biological nature of paternity. Hence blood ties were not recognized between children and relatives on their father's side. Theirs was a matrilineal group in which property was inherited through the mother's side of the family and the head of the family group was the mother's brother. At marriage, however, a woman went to live in her husband's village and hence residence was said to be patrilocal.

Anthropologists have developed a series of symbols to represent the pattern of kinship of a particular society and this can become pretty complex. Williams (1972) felt that such patterns could be divided up into six basic types depending mainly on how cousins are regarded. For example, in what is known as the Crow Indian type, the father's sister's son is called by the term for father, and the mother's brother's son is called by the term for son. While it seems unlikely that such groups actually believe that their cousins are either their fathers or sons, the kinship terms do indicate that a particular set of obligations is owed to a particular family member.

Williams argued that most kinship groups performed three functions. They provided children with a large number of models from which to acquire a knowledge of the culture. They incorporated means of deciding between the competing obligations of different family members, and finally they employed grandparents to portray the history of their group. Although these functions seemed to be observed in virtually all the cultures for which he had data, they were totally absent in industrialized urban societies. We have seen, however, how the extended family was still important in parts of this country in the nineteen-fifties, though it was much more in evidence in working-class communities than in the middle-class suburbs (Willmott and Young, 1960).

Marriage used to be thought of as serving a function of recruitment of additional members into a group of kinfolk and hence aiding their economic viability. Lévi-Strauss, however, saw marriage in a different light. He felt that marriages reduced the possibility of disharmony between opposing groups by the formation of alliances between the members of two kinship networks. When marriage occurred within the kinship network it served to bind the group together in an even more cohesive unit. This idea of the need for the formation of alliances allowed an additional explanation for one of the almost universal observances of societies: the taboo against incest.

Incest
Although virtually all societies impose a ban on sexual relationships between some family members, 'many societies do not have severe penalties for it; others practise it, and some are totally indifferent to it' (Fox, 1967). To some extent the banning of marriage relationships between family members has to be explained separately from the prohibition on sexual relations. However, that some form of alliance theory may be

125

at work for at least some societies is indicated by the fact that taboo groups may be extended to include individuals who have no traceable ancestors in common (Benedict, 1935). In fact amongst some Australian groups the taboo group became so wide that the only solution was for couples to elope and then sheepishly return once their transgression had diminished in importance.

Another explanation for the observance of an incest taboo has invoked the notion that 'familiarity breeds contempt'. However, at least in terms of their physical development, children change far more than marriage partners, which might suggest that parent-child sexual relationships ought to be more common than those between husbands and wives! Several societies adopt marriage between cousins as the most favoured situation and this would preclude an explanation in terms of the harmful effects of inbreeding. The notion that there is an instinctive avoidance of sexual relations with close kin would seem equally unlikely. When compared with animals lower down the evolutionary scale, humans seem to have far less reliance on instinctive behaviour, and there is no other animal group which practises avoidance of sexual relations with kin. On balance then it seems that the incest taboo has become embodied in the cultures of the world probably because of a common function in promoting cooperation between groups.

The varieties of family life

A variety of different patterns of family life have also evolved in 'Westernized' nations among different groups to meet the challenge of childrearing. This diversity has at times shattered some of the notions that there is only one type of family that is conducive to the mental health of children. Other groups can still be regarded as experiments in living with an, as yet, uncertain outcome.

The Kibbutz
The Kibbutz in Israel is an agricultural community of between three and five hundred people. They have adopted a

communal method of childrearing in which children live away from their parents in a children's house. However they spend a period of each evening with their parents during which they receive their undivided attention. Kibbutzim have been used as a natural experiment on the effects of differing child-rearing practices.

However, groups of urban American and English children have an environment that differs in a number of ways from that of Kibbutz children and it is extremely difficult to attribute psychological differences between these and Kibbutz-reared children solely to childrearing differences.

As Levine (1970) has concluded, from the vast number of published works on Kibbutz upbringing, all they have shown is that collective infant and childrearing need not inflict obvious damage on the intelligence and mental health of individuals. Children are reared who are not only capable of fully enjoying their lives, but who are also, on the whole, interested in perpetuating the style of life of their parents.

Communes

It has become fairly popular in recent years to look at the growing number of communes in England and America, but the major effect of the research has possibly been on the researchers rather than in terms of the results. In his book, *The New Families* (1972), Speck claims to have been converted to an admiration of the way of life of the young people who, through their use of drugs and in their struggle to find alternative ways of life, were performing a useful experiment for future generations. However, later in the book he mentions that the average duration of the communes he studied was three months, and that most of the young people left their groups to enter conventional employment. The groups that tended to persist most were those that shared a common political aim. However in many respects the communes described by Speck seem little different from student flats.

In a rather different category are studies of the efforts of communes in Germany to provide real alternatives to the family and these are reported in Dreitzel's (1973) book. Their aim is to rationalize the organization of consumption, relieve the pressure for emotional support for their members, share in household chores, and 'liberate' each other from sex roles. Although parents retain a strong link to their children, there is a determination to allow the children to be part of the adult culture. Infantile sexuality, as it has been in the past, and as it is for the Balinese, is not only tolerated but actally affirmed. Some groups permit child-adult sex play. These communes have run up against a common problem in that they have tended to have many more adults than children. They also present a particular challenge to children who are given an atypical upbringing in a culture dominated by other child-rearing approaches.

One-parent families

It is worth taking a glimpse at the research on one-parent, usually fatherless, families since they share a problem with other deviant family groups. In our society children are expected to live with a father and mother, and one might predict that they would suffer 'relative deprivation' as a result. This is apart from any harmful effects that one would argue from father absence. In societies in which men are not tied to any particular woman the culturally-sanctioned practice would appear to have no drastically disturbing effect. In a careful review of the literature Herzog and Sudia (1972) felt that there was no firm evidence to indicate that fatherlessness produced disturbance. They felt that the 'fatherless family should be studied as a form in its own right, not as the absence of true familiness'. Male role models for the boys were not as absent as some people have suggested. They noted, too, that any ill effects could be related equally to the increased economic hardship that many such families faced. Clearly in a society in which there is bound to be a wide variation in the life styles of individuals the appropriate question may not be 'how does this style of life harm the people concerned?' but 'how can we reduce the possibly harmful effects of pressure to conformity?'

Summary

In this chapter I have surveyed the life styles and patterns of development of different groups in different societies. I have looked too at some of the problems which are involved in their study. I have opted for a detailed account of a few groups rather than attempting a total survey of all the groups that are known. I have done this because I have felt that other surveys sometimes fail to give a glimpse of how others must experience their own lives. In searching for differences between attitudes and interests of men and women my view has been that there is so much possible overlap between the groups that general differences tell us little about the lives of individuals. They certainly do not permit us to regard a woman or man who adopts some of the features which have been commonly ascribed to the opposite sex as psychologically maladjusted. The whole area of kinship interactions is a fascinating subject which can be understood in the context of a total social pattern. At a recent American conference on Women's Liberation, black African women looked on incredulously as Western women decried the family as the basis of their subjugation. Family patterns for them were part of a pattern of social relationships that transcended the battleground of the sexes.

6
Nature and change in man

In this book I have been stressing the diversity in the development of people and have looked for the areas of study most likely to throw light on this diversity. Some people have been so impressed with the variety of possible human behaviour that they have doubted whether there are any biological limits to development at all. Malson (1964) was considerably influenced by the lives of children who were brought up by animals outside the influence of human culture. He commented: 'The idea that man has no nature is now beyond dispute. He has or rather is a history.' Had he been struck dead by a thunderbolt at the moment he wrote that, his next of kin would have been only too aware that Lucien Malson is only human like the rest of us. Humans do have biological limits, and their death is the most profound of these. Nevertheless the extent to which cultures can impose their own pattern of development on the biological structure of man is remarkable.

In searching for the regularities in childrearing practices between different societies, M. E. Goodman (1964) came up with two. Children need affection and need to be guided or trained by an older person. Some people seem to be so delighted when they come across a universal feature of societies that they overemphasize its importance. In contrast to Goodman's modest offering, Whiting and Child (1953) had this to say:

> Child Training the world over is in certain important respects identical ... in all societies the helpless infant, getting his food by nursing at his mother's breast and having digested it, freely evacuating the waste products, exploring his genitals, biting and kicking at will, must be changed into a responsible adult, obeying the rules of society ... child training everywhere seems to be, in considerable part, concerned with problems which arise from universal characteristics of the human infant and from universal characteristics of infantile behaviour

This seems to me to be merely saying that the 'training' or socialization of the unsocialized infant is a universal feature of all societies. It says less than Goodman, who also regards the child as in need of affection or attention.

It is instructive to see in what ways simple biological limits impose regularities on a society. The practice of childrearing produces a particular pattern of relationships between the individuals of a society. Their early infant dependence on caretakers usually means that others must bear responsibility for providing for them, as does the later frailty of old people. All societies too must develop some system of producing food and designing homes, and the conditions under which they live and acquire food will also affect the way in which they train their young. Death itself promotes a need for the constant replacement of the functions that old people have served by younger members of their group and necessitates the training of young people for their new roles. It is simple facts like these that led Piddington (1957) to conclude that because people have certain universal biological needs and tendencies, human societies tend to take on a universal pattern.

Whether one is impressed with the regularity or diversity of societies or people depends on one's interests. I suggested that the most pertinent way of deciding on the extent of the similarities between peoples and groups is in terms of the way they experience their own lives. One can imagine Malinowski

131

looking down from his status as a member of the Polish upper class and wondering how deeply he could share in the lives of the Trobriand islanders. Or perhaps we should try to place ourselves inside the thoughts of Anne Moody when she remarked 'sometimes mama would bring us the white family's left-overs, it was the best food I had ever eaten. That was when I discovered white folks ate different from us. They had all kinds of different food with meat and all. We always had just beans and bread'.

I am often struck by the egocentricity of statements which maintain that a particular aspect of behaviour is part of human nature. We grow up in an interaction with our culture and environment. When someone makes a statement about the nature of man, then they are making a claim about the past and the future for all people for all time. If we maintain, for example, that aggression is part of human nature then we are suggesting that there never has been nor ever will be a society which is capable of managing its affairs harmoniously and transmitting its culture from generation to generation. I cannot claim to be a fortune-teller, but in view of some of the practices which societies manage to transmit this does not seem to be entirely beyond the bounds of possibility. It is part of our nature that we cannot be certain of the future of our descendants.

While we can be sure that humans are limited by their biological nature it is also certain that they are part of nature. Darwin attempted to put people in their place when he viewed them as involved in achieving an adaptation to their environment like every other living thing. However the implications of this notion have been very slow in filtering through to the individuals of Western society. Commenting on the peoples of other parts of the world Lévi-Strauss suggested that 'those which have best protected their distinctive character appear to be societies predominantly concerned with persevering in their existence. The way in which they exploit the environment guarantees both a modest standard of living and the conservation of natural resources.' In looking at the value orientation of different societies Kluckholm and Strodtbeck

(1961) incorporated as one of their central variables whether a society regards itself as subjugated by nature, as living in harmony with it, or as achieving mastery over the natural environment. Western society has clearly attempted to master nature and the continued pursuance of this value will bring eventual disaster.

There is no shortage of books or television programmes about the possibility or probability of an ecological crisis. As Black (1970) has pointed out, even the use of the word crisis suggests that if we ride out the present storm everything will return to normal. There is, of course, little point in attempting to predict the precise point when life will become intolerable. However, the major social change that we require in our society is a shift from a present view of mastery to one of harmony with nature. It may be a comfort that there are other societies who have embodied this notion within their cultural system. Willis (1974) looked at the relationship between men and animals in three African societies, each one representing a different value orientation towards the natural world. One group, the Nuer, had incorporated the value of equality. Perhaps we have a greater need to import some of the successes of other cultural systems than to export further the excesses of our own. Humans can only develop in the context of an environment that enables them to thrive.

Further Reading

Chapter 2
Bronfenbrenner, U. (1970) *Two Worlds of Childhood*. Harmondsworth: Penguin.
Elkin, F. and Handel, G. (1972) *The Child and Society: The Process of Socialization*. New York: Random House.
Malson, L. (1964) *Wolf Children and the Wild Boy of Aveyron*. London: New Left Books.
Rutter, M. (1972) *Maternal Deprivation Reassessed*. Harmondsworth: Penguin.
Schaffer, H. R. (1971) *The Growth of Sociability*. Harmondsworth: Penguin.

Chapter 3
Freud, S. (1930) *Civilisation and its Discontents*. London: Hogarth Press.
Kagan, J. and Moss, H. (1962) *From Birth to Maturity: A Study in Psychological Development*. New York and London.
Mischel, W. (1968) *Personality and Assessment*. New York: Wiley.
Warr, P. B. (ed.) *Thought and Personality*. Harmondsworth: Penguin.

Chapter 4
Aries, P. (1962) *Centuries of Childhood*. Harmondsworth: Penguin.

Berg, H. H. Van der (1961) *The Changing Nature of Man*. New York: Delta Books.

Fletcher, R. (1962) *The Family and Marriage in Britain*. Harmondsworth: Penguin.

Keniston, K. (1968) *Young Radicals: Notes on Committed Youth*. New York: Harcourt.

Rowbotham, S. (1973) *Hidden from History*. London: Pluto Press.

Willmott, P. (1966) *Adolescent Boys of East London*. Harmondsworth: Penguin.

Chapter 5

Barnouw, V. (1973) *Culture and Personality*. Homewood, Ill.: Dorsey Press.

Benedict, R. (1935) *Patterns of Culture*. London: Routledge and Kegan Paul.

Dreitzel, P. (ed.) (1973) *Childhood and Socialization*. New York: Collier-Macmillan.

Fox, R. (1967) *Kinship and Marriage*. Harmondsworth: Penguin.

Goodman, M. E. (1964) *The Culture of Childhood*. New York: Teachers College Press.

Hutt, C. (1972) *Males and Females*. Harmondsworth: Penguin.

Mead, M. (1949) *Male and Female: A Study of the Sexes in a Changing World*. New York: Dell.

Williams, T. R. (1972) *Introduction to Socialization: Human Culture Transmitted*. St Louis: Mosby.

Chapter 6

Black, J. (1970) *The Dominion of Man*. Edinburgh: Edinburgh University Press.

Dubos, R. (1968) *So Human an Animal*. London: Abacus Books.

Lorenz, K. (1974) *Civilized Man's Eight Deadly Sins*. London: Methuen.

References and Name Index

The numbers in italics following each entry refer to page numbers within this book.

Ainsworth, M. D. (1964) Patterns of attachment behaviour shown by infant interaction with his mother. *Merrill-Palmer Quarterly* 10: 51–8. *39*

Ainsworth, M. D. (1967) *Infancy in Uganda: Infant Care and the Growth of Love.* Baltimore: Johns Hopkins. *105*

Anderson, J. (1956) Child development: an historical perspective. *Child Development* 27: 181–96. *73*

Aries, P. (1962) *Centuries of Childhood.* Harmondsworth: Penguin. *75, 83, 84, 96*

Bailyn, L. (1959) Mass media and children: a study of exposure habits and cognitive effects. *Psychological Monograph* 73 (471): 1–39. *53*

Bandura, A. (1969) Social learning theory of identificatory processes. In D. A. Goslin (ed.) *Handbook of Socialisation Theory and Research.* Chicago: Rand McNally. *45*

Barnouw, V. (1973) *Culture and Personality.* Homewood, Ill.: Dorsey Press. *108*

Beauvoir, S. de. (1949) *The Second Sex.* London: Jonathan Cape. *118*

Benedict, R. (1935) *Patterns of Culture.* London: Routledge and Kegan Paul. *109*

Benedict, R. (1938) Continuity and discontinuity in cultural conditioning. In M. Mead and M. Wolfenstein (eds) *Childhood in Contemporary Cultures.* Chicago: University of Chicago Press. *111*

Berg, J. H. Van der (1961) *The Changing Nature of Man*. New York: Delta Books. *73*

Bernstein, B. (1964) Elaborated and restricted codes: their social origins and some consequences. *American Anthropologist 66* (6): 55–69. *41*

Black, J. (1970) *The Dominion of Man*. Edinburgh: Edinburgh University Press. *133*

Booth, A. (1972) Sex and social participation. *Journal of American Sociology 37*: 183–93. *124*

Bossard, J. and Boll, E. (1966) *Sociology of Child Development*. New York: Harper and Row. *20*

Bowlby, J. (1953) *Child Care and the Growth of Love*. Harmondsworth: Pelican. *42, 49*

Bowlby, J. (1969) *Attachment and Loss, 1*. London: Hogarth Press. *41*

Brecher, F. (1970) *The Sex Researchers*. London: Andre Deutsch. *121*

Brim, O. (1960) Personality as role-learning. In I. Iscoe and H. Stevenson (eds) *Personality Development in Children*. Austin: University of Texas Press. *58*

Bronfenbrenner, U. (1970) *Two Worlds of Childhood*. Harmondsworth: Penguin. *47*

Bryan, J. and Test, M. (1967) Models and helping: naturalistic studies in aiding behaviour. *Journal of Personality and Social Psychology VI*: 400–07. *46*

Bullock, Alan (Chmn) (1975) *A Language for Life*. London: HMSO. *98*

Child, I. (1954) Socialization. In G. Lindsay (ed.) *Handbook of Social Psychology*. Reading, Mass.: Addison-Wesley. *26*

Cohen, Y. A. (1964) *The Transition From Childhood to Adolescence*. Chicago: Aldine. *116*

Cooper, D. (1971) *The Death of the Family*. Harmondsworth: Penguin. *94*

Cummings, E. and Henry, W. (1961) *Growing Old: The Process of Disengagement*. New York: Basic Books. *66*

D'Andrade, R. G. (1966) Sex difference and cultural institutions. In E. E. Maccoby (ed.) *The Development of Sex Differences*. Stanford, Calif.: Stanford University Press. *110*

Danziger, K. (1971) *Socialization*. Harmondsworth: Penguin. *103*

Darwin, C. (1859) *The Origin of the Species*. (Several editions available, e.g. London: Dent, Everyman's edition.)

Davis, K. (1947) Final note on a case of extreme isolation. *American Journal of Sociology 52*: 432–7. *48*

Dreitzel, P. (ed.) (1973) *Childhood and Socialization*. New York: Collier-Macmillan. *127*

Dubos, R. (1968) *So Human An Animal*. London: Abacus Books. *17, 76*

Elkin, F. and Handel, G. (1972) *The Child and Society: The Process of Socialization*. New York: Random House. *26*

Elkin, F. and Westley, W. (1955) The myth of adolescent culture. *American Sociological Review 20* (6): 680–4. *89*

Erikson, E. (1950) *Childhood and Society*. Harmondsworth: Pelican. *68*

Ervin, S. (1964) Language and TAT content in bi-linguals. *Journal of Abnormal and Social Psychology 68*: 500–07. *105*

Festinger, H. (1959) *A Theory of Cognitive Dissonance*. London: Tavistock. *117*

Firestone, S. (1972) *The Dialectic of Sex*. London: Paladin. *30, 84*

Fletcher, R. (1962, 3rd ed. 1973) *The Family and Marriage in Britain*. Harmondsworth: Penguin. *96*

Fortune, R. (1939) Arapesh warfare. *American Anthropologist 41*: 22–41. *108*

Fox, R. (1967) *Kinship and Marriage*. Harmondsworth: Penguin. *71, 125*

Freud, S. (1930) *Civilisation and its Discontents*. London: Hogarth Press. *57*

Friedl, E. (1962) *Vasilika: A village in modern Greece*. New York: Rinehart and Winston. *102*

Gewirtz, J. L. (1969) Mechanisms of social learning: some roles of stimulation and behaviour in early human development. In D. A. Goslin (ed.) *Handbook of Socialization: Theory and Research*. Chicago: Rand McNally. *25*

Gladwin, T. and Sarason, S. (1953) *Truk: Man in Paradise*. New York: Viking Fund Publications in Anthropology. *104*

Goodman, M. E. (1964) *The Culture of Childhood*. New York: Teachers College Press, Columbia University. *93, 130*

Goodman, M. E. (1967) *The Individual and Culture*. Illinois: Homewood. *112*

Goffman, E. (1961) *Asylums*. Harmondsworth: Penguin. *52*

Hall, G. (1904) *Adolescence*. New York and London: Appleton. *88*

Hampson, J. L. (1965) Determinants of psychosexual orientation. In F. A. Beach (ed.) *Sex and Behaviour*. New York: Wiley. *120*

Herzog, F. and Sudia, C. (1972) Fatherless homes: a review of the research. In I. Weiner and D. Elkind (eds) *Readings in Child Development*. New York: Wiley. *128*

Himelweit, H. F. (1958) *Television and the Child*. London: Oxford University Press. *35*

Hollis, A. C. (1909) *The Nandi*. London: Oxford University Press. *114*

Holt, J. (1974) *Escape from Childhood*. New York: Dutton. *38*

Hutt, C. (1972) *Males and Females*. Harmondsworth: Penguin. *75, 118, 119*

Illich, I. (1972) *Deschooling Society*. London: Calder and Boyars. *76*

Illich, I. (1975) *Medical Nemesis: The Expropriation of Health*. London: Calder and Boyars. *82*

Janeway, E. (1972) *Man's World, Woman's Place*. London: Michael Joseph. *75, 83*

Kandel, D. B. and Lesser, G. S. (1972) *Youth in Two Worlds: United States and Denmark*. San Francisco: Jossey-Bass. *100*

Kagan, J. and Moss, H. (1962) *From Birth to Maturity: A Study in Psychological Development*. New York and London: Wiley. *60, 63, 64*

Keniston, K. (1968) *Young Radicals: Notes on Committed Youth*. New York: Harcourt. *74, 91*

Klein, J. (1965) *Samples from English Culture*. London: Routledge and Kegan Paul. *123*

Kluckholm, E. and Strodtbeck, F. (1961) *Variations in Value Orientations*. Illinois: Evanston. *132*

Kohlberg, L. (1969) Stage and sequence: the cognitive developmental approach to socialization. In D. A. Goslin *Handbook of Socialization: Theory and Research*. Chicago: Rand McNally. *22*

Labov, W. (1970) The study of language in its social context. In P. Gigioli (ed.) *Language and Social Context*. Harmondsworth: Penguin. *41*

Landauer, T. K. and Whiting, J. W. M. (1964) Infantile stimulation and adult stature of human males. *American Anthropologist* 66: 1007–28. *16*

Laslett, P. (1965) *The World We have Lost*. London: Methuen. *83*

Lévi-Strauss, C. (1967) *The Scope of Anthropology*. London: Jonathan Cape. *103, 106, 110, 125*

Levine, R. (1970) Cross-cultural study in child psychology. In P. H. Mussen (ed.) *Carmichael's Manual of Child Psychology* 2. New York: Wiley. *101, 103, 110, 127*

Linton, R. (1939) Marquesan culture. In A. Kardiner (ed.) *The Individual and His Society*. New York: Columbia University Press. *109*

Linton, R. (1942) Age and sex categories. *American Sociological Review* 7: 589–603. *18, 109*

Lowe, G. (1972) *The Growth of Personality*. Harmondsworth: Penguin. *19*

MacIver, R. M. and Page, C. N. (1957) *Society*. New York: Macmillan. *94*

Malinowski, B. (1967) *A Diary in the Strict Sense of the Word*. London: Routledge and Kegan Paul. *106, 107, 124*

Malson, L. (1964) *Wolf Children and the Wild Boy of Aveyron*.

London: New Left Books. *48, 130*

Mead, M. (1928) *Coming of Age in Samoa*. Harmondsworth: Penguin. *11, 109*

Mead, M. (1930) *Growing Up in New Guinea*. Harmondsworth: Penguin. *11, 113*

Mead, M. (1935) *Sex and Temperament in Three Primitive Societies*. New York: Dell. *108, 118, 122*

Mead, M. (1949) *Male and Female: A Study of the Sexes in a Changing World*. New York: Dell. *108, 122*

Mead, M. and Wolfenstein, M. (eds) (1955) *Childhood in Contemporary Cultures*. Chicago: University of Chicago Press. *113*

Mead, M. (1973) *Black Berry Winter: My Earlier Years*. London and Sydney: Angus and Robertson. *107*

Mischel, W. (1968) *Personality and Assessment*. New York: Wiley. *60*

Mischel, W. (1973) Continuity and change in personality. In D. Charles and W. Looft (eds) *Readings in Psychological Development Through Life*. New York: Holt Rinehart and Winston. *60*

Money, J. and Ehrhardt, A. A. (1968) Prenatal hormonal exposure: possible effects on behaviour in man. In R. B. Michael (ed.) *Endocrinology and Human Behaviour*. London: Oxford University Press. *120*

Moody, A. (1970) *Coming of Age in Mississippi. An Autobiography*. New York: Delta. *11, 132*

Musgrave, P. W. (1968) *Society and Education in England Since 1800*. London: Methuen. *97*

Musgrove, F. (1966) *The Family, Education and Society*. London: Routledge and Kegan Paul. *96*

Musgrove, F. (1967) Childhood and adolescence. In *Educational Implications of Social and Economic Change*. London: HMSO. *89*

Nash, J. (1970) *Developmental Psychology, a Psycho-Biological Approach*. New Jersey: Prentice-Hall. *25, 118*

Neugarten, B. and Datan, N. (1973) In P. B. Baltes and K. W. Shaie (eds) *Life Span Developmental Psychology. Personality and Socialization*. New York and London: Academic Press. *13, 66*

Neugarten, B. and Paterson, W. (1957) A study of the American age grade system. In *Proceedings of the Fourth Congress of the International Association of Gerontology, 3*: 497–502. *65*

Newson, J. and Newson, E. (1974) Cultural aspects of childrearing in the English speaking world. In M. Richards (ed.) *The Integration of a Child into a Social World*. Cambridge: Cambridge University Press. *123*

Nimkoff, M. F. (1963) Changing family relationships of older people in the United States during the last forty years. In C. G. Vedder (ed.) *Gerontology: A Book of Readings*. Springfield, Ill.: Charles C. Thomas. *21*

Parsons, T. (1949) *The Social System*. Glencoe, Ill.: Free Press. *58*

Phillips, B. S. (1969) *Sociology, Social Structure and Change*. New York: Macmillan. *99*

Piddington, R. (1957) *An Introduction to Social Anthropology, II*. Edinburgh: Oliver and Boyd. *131*

Pinchbeck, I. and Hewitt, M. (1969) *Children in English Society, I*. London: Routledge and Kegan Paul. *77*

Plumb, J. H. (1950) *England in the Eighteenth Century*. London: Penguin. *77*

Power, E. (1924) *Medieval People*. London: Methuen. *95*

Rheingold, H. (1966) The development of social behaviour in the human infant. *Society for Research in Child Development, Monograph 31* (5): 1–18. *40*

Rheingold, H. L. (1969) The social and socializing infant. In D. A. Goslin (ed.) *Handbook of Socialization: Theory and Research*. Chicago: Rand McNally. *37*

Rheingold, H. and Eckerman, F. (1973) Fear of the stranger: a critical examination. In *Advances in Child Development and Behaviour 8*: 186–219. *42*

Rosenberg, B. (1968) Family interaction effects on masculinity and femininity. *Journal of Personal and Social Psychology 8*: 117–20. *121*

Rowbotham, S. (1973) *Hidden from History*. London: Pluto Press. *77*

Rubin, I. (1973) The sexless older years – a socially harmful stereotype. In D. Charles and W. Looft (eds) *Readings in Psychological Development through Life*. New York: Holt Rinehart and Winston. *66*

Rutter, M. (1972) *Maternal Deprivation Reassessed*. Harmondsworth: Penguin. *49*

Ryerson, A. J. (1961) Medical advice on child rearing, 1550–1900. *Harvard Educational Review 31*: 302–33. *85*

Sangster, P. (1963) *Pity my Simplicity*. London: Epworth Press. *79*

Schaffer, H. R. (1971) *The Growth of Sociability*. Harmondsworth: Penguin. *42*

Schaffer, H. R. and Emerson, P. E. (1964) The development of social attachments in infancy. *Society for Research in Child Development Monograph 29* (3): 3–75. *42*

Sears, R., Rav, L. and Albert, R. (1965) *Identification and Child Rearing*. Stanford, Calif.: Stanford University Press. *121*

Sears, R., Maccoby, E. and Levin, H. (1957) *Patterns of Child Rearing*. Illinois: Evanston. *121*

Sillitoe, A. (1970) *Britain in Figures*. Harmondsworth: Penguin. *81*

Speck, R. (1972) *The New Families*. London: Tavistock. *127*

Spitz, R. A. (1950) Anxiety in infancy. A study of its manifestations in the first year of life. *International Journal of Psychoanalysis* *31*: 138–43. *47*

Storr, A. (1968) *Human Aggression.* Harmondsworth: Penguin. *119*

Tanner, J. M. (1968) Earlier maturation in man. *Scientific American.* *218*: 21–7. *14*

Tiger, L. (1970) *Men in Groups.* New York: Random House. *123*

Walters, R. and Thomas, E. (1963) Enhancement of punitiveness by visual and audiovisual displays. *Canadian Journal of Psychology XVIII* (2): 244–55.

Wax, M. L. (1972) Tenting with Malinowski. *Journal of American Sociology 37*: 1–15. *107*

Whiting, J. (1964) Effect of climate on cultural practices. In W. H. Goodenough (ed.) *Explorations in Cultural Anthropology.* New York: McGraw-Hill. *117*

Whiting, J. and Child, I (1953) *Child Training and Personality: A Cross-Cultural Study.* New Haven, Conn.: Yale. *103, 131*

Williams, T. R. (1972) *Introduction to Socialization: Human Culture Transmitted.* St. Louis: Mosby. *116, 124*

Willis, R. (1975) *Man and Beast.* London: Paladin. *133*

Willmott, P. (1966) *Adolescent Boys of East London.* Harmondsworth: Penguin. *53*

Willmott, P. and Young, M. (1960) *Family and Class in a London Suburb.* London: Routledge and Kegan Paul. *125*

Wilson, M. (1951) *Good Company.* London: Oxford University Press. *114*

Witkin, H. A. (1965) Psychological differentiation. In P. B. Warr (ed.) *Thought and Personality.* Harmondsworth: Penguin. *63*

Wolfenstein, M. (1953) Trends in infant care. *American Journal of Orthopsychiatry 23*: 120–30. *85*

Wolff, P. H. (1969) The natural history of crying and other vocalization in early infancy. In B. M. Foss (ed.) *Determinants of Infant Behaviour 4.* London: Methuen. *39*

Yarrow, M. R., Campbell, J. D. and Burton, R. V. (1968) *Child-rearing: An Enquiry into Research and Methods.* San Francisco: Jossey-Bass. *59*

Young, M. and Willmott, P. (1957) *Family and Kinship in East London.* Harmondsworth: Penguin. *96*

Subject Index

144